"The first time I met Regina I was impressed by her charisma and sharp and pragmatic thinking. As a coach cum consultant, she guided me through my next professional phase. The reader of this book will have the chance to be guided by the pragmatic, direct and intuitive advice of a professional condensing and combining a longstanding executive experience with international companies, the Asian determination and the sensibility of a woman who managed to emerge in a very competitive environment through her professional skills and winning interpersonal relationships."

Nicola Battalora
CEO, BSI Bank Limited, Luxembourg SA

"Regina is a true practitioner in the art of relationship selling. Using a very compelling and intuitive approach, she has masterfully distilled her years of experience into a practice guide for building and managing rewarding relationships. The perceptive reader will discover rich insights throughout the book as Regina dissects and dispels common misconceptions of consultative selling, and offering a uniquely Asian context to her art."

Gordon Lam
Vice President—APJ IT Transformation Services
SAP Asia Pacific Japan

"Regina understands the different market needs and the call for localization. Her creative problem solving skills when tasked with new challenges and her ability to adapt across industry helped bring clarity to many problems. She possesses an uncanny ability to talk to the point, was able to express her thoughts in a colloquial yet impressionable manner, and always had a fiery passion when it came to work. Her time with Schlumberger, where the challenges were diverse and steep, had certainly shaped her views and given her the confidence to share her experiences. Her good interpersonal skills should make team learning a fun and memorable experience."

Goh Hock
Worldwide President
SchlumbergerSema, Network Solutions Worldwide

F.I.R.E.F.L.Y.

Consultative Engagement

How to build trust and credibility with customers?

REGINA CHUA

To order additional copies of this book, contact:
Xlibris Corporation
1-888-795-4274
www.Xlibris.com
Orders@Xlibris.com
63086

For Peter, my husband
For Nicolette, Reuben and Russell, my children

May your life be filled with health and hope.
May your faith and courage lift you higher than your challenges.
And may the joy and peace of trusting God live in your heart forever.

Contents

Introduction

FIREFLY is a systematic but simple model—based on years of research and experience—that will help you reach your full potential. If you apply the FIREFLY principles, they'll transform your sales engagement, yield improved results, and change the way you connect with and relate to people forever.

Having worked in the international corporate arena for years, I've seen both success and failure stories. I've witnessed how powerful sales professionals build strong relationships and achieve or surpass their sales goals. I've also seen technically excellent sales professionals fail to create a connection with prospects and, as a result, lose sales they almost had.

The selling landscape has become more competitive than ever. Whether you're working in commercial, retail, or a non-profit organization, the ability to establish credibility with your customers or stakeholders is critical to success. Gone are the days of empathetic management willing to reduce annual sales objectives during tough times. Many today see that move as almost fatal, perceiving that it would open the doors to complacency.

The adage "What you don't know, you can't manage" is the reason behind the worldwide proliferation of self-improvement tools and fire-walking boot camps. What I'm going to tell you today is that, no matter where you are in your career, if you don't harness your strengths, you're going to miss out on developing your true potential.

If you've picked up a copy of this book, you're clearly interested in becoming a more effective sales professional. I have good news for you: if you can harness your ability to engage with customers, they'll trust you, and you in turn will achieve a win-win outcome for both parties.

One of those key strengths is the ability to seamlessly get along with everybody you meet. Yes, you have it in you! Within you lies the ability to break ice quickly and create an instant connection with prospects.

When I took the leap of faith to start my own consultancy firm, I used the FIREFLY model as a tool to engage and educate during workshops. Participants of the workshops found a heightened awareness of themselves. Seasoned professionals gained fresh insights into their strengths and how to leverage on their strengths, and sales newbies found the model intuitive enough to consciously use to build rapport and trust.

No matter what type of organization you're involved in, FIREFLY is designed to help you see that there is an *intentional approach* to consultative engagement. You'll begin to uncover ideas and options to help you become far more successful in your interactions with customers than you ever thought possible!

I have been fascinated and greatly encouraged by the feedback that I have received from my clients about how simple and powerful FIREFLY is. My wish for you is that FIREFLY will be practical and relevant for you. No, let's rephrase that—I know it will be.

Chapter 1

Flex

Why is it that some people seem to be able to get along with everyone even when they are as different as chalk and cheese? The fact that they do is good news for folks like me who weren't born with natural charisma. Did you know that genuine engagement comes from the quality of your connection to another person? People get along with one another when both of them are on the same wavelength.

Is It about the X Factor?

Raymond, a senior sales manager, was envied by everyone because he could become a chameleon in different situations. Even when dealing with the toughest customers, he seemed to have the uncanny ability to start conversations and melt the chill in the room.

Regardless of who he was dealing with, he was effortlessly able to create a connection; and customers would warm up to him quickly or, if they were angry, calm down fast when he was managing their demands. When asked about this seemingly effortless ability, he simply answered that he was just being himself and couldn't pinpoint anything specific. All he could reckon is that it probably had something to do with his strong listening skills.

Therese, on the other hand, was a different story altogether when it came to customer management. Known as one of the brightest and most industrious people in her office, she'd go the extra mile to understand her abilities, the competition, and the value that the customer could realize. But unfortunately, no matter what she did, she was always poorly rated in the annual customer survey.

Customers pointed out that Therese, though industrious and committed, was not a strategic key account manager; and they found her to be too set in her ways. As much as they agreed that she was a good worker, they found her to be brash and direct in wanting things done her way and always focused on the things that mattered to her rather than what mattered to them. Sadly, Therese couldn't understand why her clients had that perception of her despite all her hard work. She boiled it down to a lack of chemistry.

If you're like many sales professionals who need to stand out from the competition, you know that besides selling the value of your organization to customers and prospects, you need to become a pivotal value-added element too, because people tend to buy you before they buy your wares.

But how do you achieve that likeability factor?

Raymond is blessed with the elusive X-factor personality that others could only dream about. Therese has the problem of not being able to relate to anyone despite giving it her best. Even with these two very different personalities, both Raymond and Therese have something in common—neither party knows what they did or didn't do to evoke their respective responses from the people around them.

Addressing that lack of self-awareness is the beginning of the FIREFLY model.

Flex—the *F* in FIREFLY

The Golden Rule and the Platinum Rule

In the Bible, the Golden Rule talks about treating others the way you want to be treated. If I want to be treated nicely, then I should treat others nicely. If I want to be respected, then I must respect others too; and if I want to be indulged in a relaxed conversation with prospects, then I should start all introductions with an easygoing opener.

While the Golden Rule hinges on the fairness of treatment between two people, it also helps us to have some level of empathy for others. Of course the caveat is that it only works when the other person is of the same opinion as you and wants to be treated the same way as you do. Otherwise, you may end up upsetting others and being disappointed with their response.

Can you imagine applying that Golden Rule in managing your top customers? Obviously not, because it would be a tad naive to assume that you know exactly what your top clients want and that they would agree wholeheartedly with every move you suggest. From the customer's perspective, why should they care about what you want? Who's serving who anyway?

Yes, it's true—"The customer is king!" And that means it's all about him and satisfying his needs. He decides if he wants to work with you, and he judges you by what you can do for him and not the other way around. Your opinions and preferences may be of little relevance to him. What's more, he may not even want to reciprocate on your terms at all. Remember the all-too-familiar feeling that we've surrendered the reins to the customer?

So the Golden Rule may not be particularly useful with clients.

If the Golden Rule is all about what you want and trusting that others want the same thing, then the Platinum Rule is about what your customers want. The Platinum Rule says, "Treat others the way *they* want to be treated." Now it's not just about you anymore, but it's all about the other party.

As Flexible as Play-Doh

Let's talk about the first step to consultative engagement: Flex. Flexing is an essential interpersonal skill that helps you jump right onto the right bandwidth with another person, even if both of you are perfect strangers.

Flexing is the ability to adjust the way you communicate to other peoples' personality and conversation preference. When you flex, it means that you consciously observe the personality of the other and adjust your style so both of you feel as if you're on the same wavelength. The topics discussed may vary, but the area of focus and the elements in the conversation will seem to stack up pretty well. When you flex, the customer feels that you're getting his drift and giving him what he wants. Your goal is to be as flexible as Play-Doh.

Let's come back to the case of Raymond and how he applies the skill of flexing.-Raymond has the unwitting ability to adjust the way he speaks and is able to angle his pitch and select the right conversation points for each different customer. Unconsciously, he is adjusting his words and the focus of his conversation to match the person he is talking to.

How does he do it? He first flexes by being a good listener and a keen observer. From his keen sense of observation, he quickly sizes up a customer and focuses on a topic he knows will appeal to the other party. He picks up nuances in their likes and dislikes—even things as small as the fact that the customer enjoys details rather than just the end point or, conversely, that they prefer cutting to the chase and skipping over the details. Each time he talks to someone, he strives to get a feel of their preferred choice of words and focus areas, and then he flexes his conversation accordingly.

His colleagues were correct when they called him a chameleon, and best of all, his customers like him because they feel that he connects to them. That's how a simple move can immediately put you on the same bandwidth as your customer.

What Could Therese Have Done Differently?

Now, let's get back to Therese, the lady who worked so hard but was oblivious to her clients' style of communication. She told me that she had once presented to a flamboyant senior executive who was talkative and loud. As she presented her ideas, beginning with a detailed explanation about her company's capabilities, the executive started to fidget, appeared impatient, and finally, bluntly suggested that she skip everything and focus on the desired results instead.

Not one to give in so easily, Therese tried to persuade the senior executive of the value of understanding the details of her presentation. Yet again, he brushed her off and repeated that he wanted to see the executive summary instead. Furious and humiliated, she had no choice but to conclude with an abrupt and concise summary. Then, expecting the meeting to be over, she sat down and began to pack her files. To her surprise, the executive wanted more clarification about the investment returns she had mentioned. Therese was puzzled because he had been bored and fidgety and kept peeking at his watch, but now he suddenly wanted to talk. What happened?

Therese had subconsciously applied the Golden Rule and treated people the way she wanted to be treated. She loved information and step-by-step processes detailed in black and white, but that didn't work for her customer, whose body language gave clear signals that he was not interested in that level of depth.

Therese failed to realize that the senior executive was a no-nonsense, goal-orientated gentleman who only wanted to hear the bottom line. But Therese, focusing only what she felt was right from her viewpoint, had totally forgotten about the customer and his preference. Unfortunately, she failed to realize that details were not his cup of tea and that by presenting to him something he did not want, she not only diluted her value to him but actually wasted his time. Therese made him impatient because she failed to adjust to his communication style.

In hindsight, what should Therese have done? Applying the Platinum Rule instead of the Golden Rule, she should have picked up on his areas of interest and recognized what he wanted out of the presentation. Recognizing that his priority was results rather than details, she should have flexed and fine-tuned her pitch based on what he wanted to hear. In order to understand him better, Therese could have sought clarification as to why he felt that was his priority. Had she flexed to his wavelength, he would have been pleased that she connected with his needs and priorities. And once that connection is established, the two-way communication would have been sealed because both parties would be on the same wavelength. Let's take a look at how Therese—and you—can become expert at flexing to people.

What Is *DISC* in DISCO?

Apart from being a good listener and a keen observer, a good way to get started flexing is to use the DISC behavioral model. The DISC model outlines four common distinct personality types, and by understanding these four personality types, you'll find it easy to identify other people's preferred communication style through their personality type.

DISC is a behavioral model based on the work of William Marston, PhD (1893-1947), and it's a popular tool used to help us understand different communication styles. With this profiling tool, Marston's research discovered that there are four major "personality styles" and that each person tends to display specific characteristics unique to that particular style. All individuals possess all four, but what differs from one to another is the dominance of each.

It's a simple model that's easy to recall and apply because there are four distinct behaviors called DISC, and it characterizes them as follows:

- **D**ominance relates to control, power, and assertiveness
- **I**nfluence relates to social situations and communication
- **S**teadiness relates to patience, persistence, and thoughtfulness
- **C**onscientiousness relates to structure and organization

I have coined the term *DISCO* as a tool to help you anticipate and respond to these four personality types. I've added the *O* to *DISC* so it becomes *DISCO* by including an application term called oscillate. Like flexing, you need to know how to oscillate with the personality type so you can feel confident with any personality type you come across.

How Do I Flex with DISCO?

Here are some tips to help you identify and oscillate according to the different DISC personalities whenever you come across them:

Dominance: People who score high in the intensity of the D-style factor are very active in dealing with problems and challenges. Direct and decisive by nature, they appear to have a strong ego and confident. Focused on bottom-line results, they place value on time and challenges to the status quo. Impersonal and authoritarian at times, they may be perceived as blunt and callous in their approach.

- Oscillate: Flex to this type by being brief, direct, and to the point. Focus on the business goals and give ideas to help them attain their goal. Focus on the logical benefits. Don't bother with storytelling and jokes. Don't make fluffy comments or general statements without evidence. Focus on the client's problem, and be ready to respond when he challenges your views.

Influence: People with high I scores influence others through talking and activity. They tend to be emotional. They are seen as charming and persuasive with a positive and enthusiastic demeanor. Talkative and impulsive, they resist conflicts and arguments and instead seek a forum for ideas. They don't particularly like details and so may overcommit or miss important facts.

- Oscillate: Flex to this type by being friendly and letting the client occupy the airtime during the conversation by sharing their ideas and views. Develop a consultative approach and ask their opinion on things. Before asking a challenging question, acknowledge and appreciate their viewpoint. Allow social time and share testimonials and success stories. Following through on the agenda, and providing interim summaries help the client stay on track.

Steadiness: People with high S-styles scores want a steady pace and security and dislike sudden change. Such personalities are mostly calm, patient, and stable in character. Unfazed and lukewarm in comments, they enjoy consensus building and teamwork. Not wanting to be in the limelight, they prefer predictability and resist change.

- Oscillate: Create an affable ambience and make them feel appreciated. Don't hurry or rush them to a decision, but provide them with clarification for tasks and be patient in uncovering their concerns. Present new ideas in a nonthreatening manner and allow time for them to be digested. Don't be confrontational—assure them of your support and reliability.

Conscientious: People with high C styles are logical and analytical and prefer to deal with black-and-white elements, such as rules, regulations, and structure. Perfectionists at times, they are demanding of self and like quality work and an ability to do it right the first time. They are cautious and systematic and seek accuracy and order with limited social interaction.

- Oscillate: Be prepared with evidence and accurate data. Define the project—including both pros and cons—and be professional when communicating. Avoid tentative words like *maybe, sometimes, I think so*, etc. Scope each task with a clear explanation of how that task fits into the big picture. Be systematic and comprehensive in dialogue, and if you have to disagree, do it diplomatically.

How Do I Apply DISCO at Work?

Let's revisit the example of Therese and her meeting with the senior executive. Observing that he began the meeting with an arm's-length approach and impatience for the bottom line, one could guess that he would be a dominant (D) personality. Soon it became even more evident that he was a dominant character as he was focused almost exclusively on result. Therese should have identified those traits and managed her pitch to cover the primary goals and outcomes to stay aligned to his preference.

Thereafter, we observed that he continued to ask for evidence, third-party endorsement, and proof of the company's performance. This is a conscientious (C) personality trait, and Therese should have calibrated and provided the relevant details he needed to validate the information.

Over time, as he got to know Therese, he became friendlier and became comfortable with casual business meetings over lunch instead of his office. As the relationship evolved and the influencing (I) personality trait came to the fore in the client's relationship with Therese, she too automatically became more casual and empathetic in such an easygoing setting, but without being aware of her own behavioral transformation.

A year after the solutions were deployed successfully, Therese's client was so comfortable with the methods used by her company that he left everything in her hands, provided that she ironed out all the standard operating procedures. The customer then evolved into a stable (S) personality and is now less adventurous than before, demanding that Therese maintain the status quo. His motto has become "If it ain't broke, don't fix it."

Unfortunately, throughout the client's behavioral evolution, Therese found herself following along and never quite knowing what was coming next. It was only blind luck that allowed her to keep the client happy. Had she understood his changing personality types, she would have taken a more proactive role and had an easier time of it.

When you flex, you become versatile and oscillate your behavior to match the communication style of your client. Why does the customer respond positively to you when you flex to them? Because you've blended into their style of communication by echoing their needs. You've made it easier for them to communicate with you.

Why *Don't* People Flex?

Apart from ignorance, many people choose not to flex because emotions and ego get in the way. While many may call it a misunderstanding, I would call it a miscommunication. It's hard to get to the topic of discussion if you can't even communicate on the same wavelength. Sadly, I've met sales professionals who never flex—and never will—because they see it as a sign of surrender to the client. But it's not. Flexing gives the sales professional a personal advantage in allowing him or her to get along with anybody, anytime.

Summary

Flexing is the ability to get conversation started on an agreeable note so that you can dive into the right topics at the right point of the dialogue. When you flex, you create open conversation and make others feel as if they can relax and relate to you. When people feel that you're speaking their language, they'll open up to you easily, and you can advance genuinely and engage the client with ease.

The ability to flex to different personalities shows your communication agility. Many times, conversations arrive at a stalemate due to personality clashes. Even the subject matter becomes secondary to the engagement itself.

By flexing, you oscillate through different personalities to get on the same wavelength, minimize misunderstanding, and maximize effective interactive dialogues. Start paying attention to the way your clients speak, and identify their style. Then flex your conversation and watch how effortlessly you can keep the customer attentive and interested in you.

By practicing DISCO and growing your self-awareness, you'll be an expert with your DISCO groove and achieve positive outcomes with any personality type.

Chapter 2

Impress

What do you think of President Barack Obama? Conventional wisdom credits about his formidable political rhetoric for his initial popularity, but it was his earnest, firm approach as well as his aura of natural charisma that won him the votes of the American people. And most of those attributes struck people within the first few moments they saw him—before he even opened his mouth.

It works the same way for you too. First impressions *do* matter. Once a customer forms his first impression of you, he will use that to determine how he wants to engage with you, and first impressions *do* matter. According to experts, we pass judgment on a person in the first thirty seconds we meet them. Once that that impression is embossed in our heads, it is difficult to shake it off.

Why a Business Suit Is Not Enough

In today's cosmopolitan society, we know enough about dressing the part and the importance of projecting an image of confidence and success. But professional image is only one part of the equation. When we're talking about engaging prospects, how can we impress them in such a way that they actually form a good impression? What else should we be looking out for?

I've worked with several organizations in which the millennial employees become middle managers in their late twenties. Having scaled quickly up the corporate ladder, I had the privilege to meet with Shania who, at the age of twenty-eight, was tasked to a regional sales position. In this position, however, Shania found that she was perceived as being too young for the position; and quite naturally, she sought to overcome the perception.

When I met her, I saw the reasons why the customer's confidence could be shaken as Shania was extremely aggressive in her gestures. By discussing and analyzing her own actions closely, she realized that she was compensating for her youthful appearance by being more aggressive than her customers felt comfortable with.

However, we also found that the initial resistance from her customers slowly ebbed away as they began to speak with her. Impressed by her knowledge of their markets, trends, and opportunities, they soon came to realize how well prepared she was in creating for them a workable solution.

During the course of our conversation, Shania expressed her dissatisfaction with the mixed-customer reviews she received. Customers who got to know her thought she was very competent, but prospects who only had an initial impression to go by were not impressed. Her overzealous drive to compensate for a lack of seniority gave others the impression that she was high-handed and arrogant—in other words, a young punk! Sadly, that was the farthest thing from the truth. Shania wanted to create a positive impression from the moment she met them. What could she do, she asked, to sharpen the way she appeared to customers?

The answer to that question is complicated but easy to grasp.

Impress—the *I* in FIREFLY

"You never get a second chance to make a first impression." It's a harsh statement, but undeniably true in today's sales environment. Unfortunately, it also means you have to hit the nail square on the head right from your very first meeting. Apart from dressing the part, what should you be looking out for?

When meeting someone for the first time, how you act and what you say affects the other person's view of who you are, and this often sets the tone for the rest of the conversation. If you want to make a good impression, besides being genuine and honest, there are ways to strengthen the impact you have. Here are a few tips that may help.

How Is a First Impression formed?

We learn from years of experience and awkward moments to refine our approach in order to create a favorable first impression on others. The projection of a first impression is a combination of our professional image and our personal interaction. The other party's first impression of us is dependent on how well we handle these two elements.

Personal Interaction

Your personal interaction shows the extent to which you present a positive impression as a person. Your sincerity is evident by the display of your attentiveness and positive signals as perceived by others. One of the ways to ensure that you're delivering the right nonverbal signals is to think of body symmetry. The beauty of symmetry demonstrates harmony, which is pleasing to the eye, so remember to show a symmetrical posture by ensuring that the left side of your body is balanced with the right side of your body. Surprisingly, sometimes people get upset and view you as disinterested or bored when your body posture is asymmetrical. When you slouch your shoulders, tilt your head or lean on one foot, your asymmetrical appearance is jarring to the other party and instinctively engenders distrust. Keep symmetry in mind when showing sincerity in your gestures.

Impress with the Four Senses

It is imperative for you to pay attention to the customer to see if he is interested in you too. Don't just speak and focus on your script. Instead, note how receptive he is by observing his nonverbal gestures.

The four senses provide a good baseline for you:

- Eye: Don't be distracted by your surroundings. Establish firm, warm eye contact with the customer. Don't dart your eyes or look down at your notes while speaking—this may be perceived as insecurity or insincerity.

- Hearing: Demonstrate your interest by nodding your head or taking notes. Avoid staring blankly at the customer or shaking your head. That expresses negativity.
- Touch: Refrain from fidgeting, covering your face, or crossing your arms when speaking—again, this may be perceived as negativity and an unwillingness to be open. Use open body language to get your client to warm up to you.
- Taste: Though not related to food, ensure that you don't purse your lip or bite your lower lip when speaking.

Having good eye contact and a symmetrical body posture will allow you to project a positive personal image. This aligning of body gestures with your speech is important. If your body gestures are incongruent to what you are saying, your message will be received with doubt from the other party.

Professional Impression

Your professional impression shows the extent to which you present a positive impression based on your profession. Your credibility will be judged according to the business acumen and knowledge you display.

There are no shortcuts in this area because you need to prepare yourself before you see a new customer. The truth of the matter is that knowing your products and your pitch is important. But what will truly strike the customer is your ability to show him that you have done your homework and are well researched.

Here, then, are the five Cs that you will pay close attention to while doing your homework. By using the Internet, business databases, and your own network, you can uncover the answers to these five Cs. Your solid understanding of your customer's organization will create a positive professional impression.

- Company: What do they do? How can you create value when you pitch your solution to them?
- Competencies: What are their distinct areas of competencies? How can you complement them?
- Competition: Who are their competitors? How can you help them differentiate themselves from their competition?

- Customers: Who are their customers? How can you improve their opportunities with their customers?
- Context: How can you help them in your current capacity?

The Elevator-Speech Introduction

We use the term *elevator speech* to describe your introduction delivered in a short and snappy fashion, as if you were in a short elevator ride with your audience.

The five Cs of preparation will help shape your introduction. Once you distribute your name business card, deliver a short, relevant self-introduction to stir the customer's interest in you.

The worst possible introduction would be to parrot what your name card already says. "My name is Nick Appleby, and I am a key account manager from Unique Solutions." Your customer can read, and he won't be impressed by wasted words. Instead, try something like "My name is Nick Appleby, and I help retail companies like yours improve traffic to their e-shops on the Internet." Make yourself relevant to the customer, and you'll gain his attention.

What's Your First Impression Like?

Putting both the personal and professional elements together will help customers form a comprehensive image of you. Here are four possible perceptions that they may get at first glance:

Tax Inspector (Professional but no personal image)	**White Knight** (Professional with a personal image)
Newspaper Boy (No professional or personal image)	**Surfer Dude** (Personal image with no professional image)

Chart: four impressions

The newspaper boy is someone who leaves virtually no impression. He is merely the backstage worker—the one responsible for ensuring newspapers are delivered each morning. The customer has little recollection and little to no impression of him.

The surfer dude is one who projects a positive personal image with his attractive appearance. However, his professional image is lacking. He is perceived as a good-looker but someone who probably lacks substance.

The tax inspector is one who may seem gawky and unrefined in his personal presentation. At work, however, he presents a perfunctory and credible appearance. Hence, he carries no personal image while projecting a distant and cold business-only image.

The white knight is one who possesses both personal and professional elements. He effortlessly communicates attentiveness and exudes charisma while actively pitching relevance to the customer. Here, we see an example of a great overall impression because both professional and personal elements are in sync.

A Case Study: What Could Shania Have Done?

Remember Shania? In the customer's eyes, Shania fell under the tax-inspector category. In Shania's case, her obliviousness to her own personal projection had a detrimental effect on her customer's receptiveness. If the customer was quiet and used small gestures, then she should have reciprocated and done likewise. If he was gregarious and spoke with great pomp and fanfare, then she should have opened her gestures and spoken with enthusiasm, without overshadowing the customer of course.

For those who are in this category, it is imperative to improve nonverbal communication skills. Try to focus on your four senses and projecting symmetry when facing your customer. This will make you seem less intimidating. It will balance your professional image to be seen as a white knight.

Summary

When you impress a customer, it goes beyond being dressed in an impeccably tailored suit. Sophisticated customers expect more, and they *will* size you up in an instant.

Impressing your customers starts with self-awareness of your personal projection. Develop a symmetrical approach in your posture, and use your four senses consciously to show your interest in the customer. In addition to that, develop your professional image and do your homework. Find out about the customer's five Cs (company, competencies, competition, customer, and context) to sharpen your personal introduction.

Chapter 3

Rapport

There is no question that we warm up to some people faster than we warm up to others. While conversation may flow easily with some, with others, it comes to a screeching halt once the introductions are completed. The difference? *Rapport.* Unless one has good rapport with one's customers, it will be an uphill task to engage the customer.

People Don't Buy from People They Don't Like

Webster's Dictionary defines rapport as "relation characterized by harmony and affinity." The connection between you and your client needs to be comfortable if your engagement is to take you anywhere.

I once entered a meeting with my CEO to meet the head of another organization. My CEO, being American, was naturally affable and friendly. He suffered a rude shock when the other CEO turned out to be a cold, distant fellow. It was obvious that the two CEOs were as different as chalk and cheese during the initial conversation, and it was no surprise to me that they never met again. But I viewed this as a wasted opportunity because I felt the other party should have put in some effort to engage my boss. Nobody broke the ice, so the conversation became perfunctory and distant. Rapport was definitely low in this case study.

My CEO is not alone in his experience. I've learnt that sometimes, we may find it challenging to build rapport in professional connections. However, it is never impossible. The onus is on us to take the first step to build rapport with our customers.

Rapport—the *R* in FIREFLY

Rapport building has to come right after first introductions because you've got to be able to carry on the dialogue. Regardless of how nervous and awkward you feel making small talk, you have to bite the bullet and just do it.

The dangers of *not* building rapport are far worse than you can imagine. Unless people feel comfortable with you, they are unlikely to be receptive and open up to you. If there is no rapport, the ambience may feel cold and transactional. If that's the case, how can the engagement be anything but superficial and futile? Obviously, that's not something you want. People need to feel connected to you because that connection brings trust. When rapport is established, a sense of trust is established. Conversely, when rapport is absent, conversation is stilted and uncomfortable.

Clean Language

One useful technique in any rapport-building session is to use the concept of clean language developed by David Grove. Using clean language can be an effective way to create deep rapport with another person.

The clean-language technique compels you to listen carefully to what the other person says so that you can use their exact words in your questions during the rapport process. This combination of active listening and using the other person's words will make the other person feel that you relate to their world easily, pleasantly surprising them and making them feel as if you both are on the same wavelength.

Clean language encourages you not to rephrase or angle his words to fit your agenda but, instead, to use the same words that the customer uses. During the rapport stage, echo his language instead of paraphrasing or replacing his ideas with yours. The rationale behind this is that the more you employ a customer's jargon and language, the more he will feel that you are appreciative of and interested in what he is saying. For example, if the customer uses the phrase "contract terms," resist the temptation to use your preferred phrase "legal obligations." Stay connected with his world and use his jargon; or else the incongruent terminology, even though it may seem a small thing to you, will dilute the connection he feels with you.

Once you are able to speak your client's language, you'll find it easier to converse and find topical issues that he is interested in. In return, you'll find that he will open up to you and may even share more than he had intended to. Why? Because you've made him feel comfortable and at ease with you. More precisely, you spoke in a manner that made him feel that you are interested in *him*.

Are Compliments and Questions Good Enough?

In the early 1990s, I learned a new lesson that my boss at the time taught me about building rapport with new customers. He reminded me to "ask questions, listen attentively, and compliment them!". Scott was a tall suave American who could instantly engage with any customer the first time they meet. At industry-trade events, he would work the room at a cocktail party and walk out with a stack of leads for me to follow up with.

Many times I would try my luck at it, but it seemed that even with the right lines, somehow I could never quite reap Scott's results. Something was amiss. Since then, I've come to realize that there is a subtle but important difference in personalities and cultures. The difference is in which areas you choose to find common ground. Finding common ground to break the ice is the crux of rapport, of course, but knowing *what* to say and *when* to say it is even more critical.

Where Do I Begin?

Let's take a look at a case study. Claus, a vibrant personality from Belgium, was placed in Asia Pacific to fulfill his job as a regional key-account manager. Meeting the head of a family-owned business, he approached the patriarch with a warm opening about the weather and traffic in his city.

Unexpectedly, the patriarch gave a noncommittal reply and followed up with the brusque question of "So what is your opinion about the economic potential in my city?" The conversation about the weather came to an abrupt end.

Initially upset by the patriarch's abruptness, Claus overcame his awkwardness by focusing on the questions asked. The patriarch was interested in his views about the business-development opportunities and continued to share his perspectives about the economic policies in his country.

The conversation thereafter took a turn for the better. The patriarch, as if impressed by Claus's knowledge of Asia, reinitiated the conversation about weather and the worsening traffic condition; and rapport began to be established. What did Claus do wrong the first time, and what did he do right the second time?

How to Build Rapport with Diverse Personalities

There are two distinct approaches to building rapport: casual and credible. What Claus unconsciously did initially was to apply casual rapport. Casual rapport makes use of topics that are related to one's lifestyle and general topic of interest. In casual rapport, you talk about the weekend, weather, sports, media, or lifestyle sections of the newspaper. This starter works well with customers whose personalities appear warm and friendly. From the DISC model, personalities that are influencing (I) or steady (S) types enjoy a conversation begun on a light and affable note. It also works well with customers who have an informal corporate culture—something quite common in American companies and young entrepreneurial start-ups.

Casual rapport creates a personal connection with the other party by connecting to a personal topic of interest. Sometimes, it's good for Monday-morning meetings as many may still be in the weekend mood. It begins the conversation at a slower pace by simply establishing a general connection between the parties.

Start on a Heavier Note with Credible Rapport

Credible rapport, in contrast, focuses on serious issues like business. Establishing credible rapport means bringing up topics like your review of a last annual report, trends in the marketplace, or even observations about the location of their office. This starter takes a corporate approach, and works well with customers whose personalities appear serious and aloof. In some Asian cultures and family-owned businesses, hierarchical and seniority status are of paramount importance, and you have to be sensitive when building rapport with the senior management. By using credible rapport, you demonstrate your respect by showing your knowledge of their business or markets.

Using the DISC model, personalities like the results-focused dominant (D) type and the analytical fact-finding (C) type may prefer this approach as they relate well to tasks and goals.

Newspapers articles from the international and local news, company results, finance and stock market reports are all helpful in researching for building credible rapport. Everything related to the business world makes a wonderful conversation starter.

Move to the Rhythm of Rapport Rumba

To move to the rhythm of rapport rumba, keep a close eye on your customer's body language and facial expressions. Listen to how they introduce themselves to get a hint about which rapport-building conversation technique is appropriate.

ALEX Technique

When building rapport, use the ALEX technique to keep the conversation engaging and interactive. ALEX stands for "ask, listen, echo, and xpress." This method enables you to participate actively instead of having a one-sided conversation.

Here's an example of the ALEX technique:

Ask: "So how do the new economic measures affect business sentiments?"

Listen: "Oh, I see." (Head nodding with eye contact.)

Echo: "So what you are saying is that cooling measure to reduce speculations . . ."

Xpress: "Could that be too drastic a step at this moment?"

Rapport conversations are blended conversations, so you've got to participate and make your comments count. Don't tire the customer by just asking questions and never giving feedback.

Because all conversations are fluid, they can easily change from casual to credible, or vice versa. From my experience and feedback from my clients, I notice two distinct differences between the way the Western and Eastern business worlds build rapport.

Credible to Casual rhythm

When building rapport with a traditional Asian client, note that they have a tendency to size you up first. By starting with credible rapport, you demonstrate your credibility in their world. Once this trust is forged, you can continue to build common ground from there.

Don't be surprised if, at the end or midway through the conversation, they initiate casual rapport by opening up with a question like "So where are you from? Do you like living in Asia?"

Generally speaking, Asian clients are more comfortable transitioning from credible to casual rapport. For them, respect comes before rapport.

Casual to Credible Rapport

Building rapport with Western clients, in contrast, may warrant a casual-rapport opener to break the ice elegantly. Starting with a credible-rapport line may appear too direct and forceful. Hence, starting on a casual note is normally the right approach to begin establishing rapport. Conversation about the weather, weekend, and especially sporting events popular in their country are all good starters.

When you use casual rapport as an opener, check to see if the customer is interested in the topic. If he shows disinterest, choose another topic instead. Use open-ended questions to avoid monotonous conversations.

Once the ice is broken, don't rush the conversation. Instead, go with the flow and enjoy the casual chat. Westerners tend to value opinions, so work your opinion into the conversation before asking a transitional question like "So how's business?" Allow the rapport to build from there.

Be flexible. People often toggle between rapport styles. However, always stay focused and interested. If you let the other party do most of the talking, remain attentive and reciprocate; you'll be a master at building rapport with any customer from now on.

Summary

Rapport building goes beyond just making small talk. Customers with different personality profiles, cultures, and corporate climates may build rapport differently.

Using the clean-language technique will assist you in connecting with the customer based on a common language. Listen and use the customer's jargon and words so that he'll feel you understand his perspective.

Building rapport can be easy when you apply ALEX in your conversations. Don't just tire the customers with questions; but instead, ask, listen, echo, and express your views too. In this way, it becomes a two-way conversation for both parties

Prepare ahead before the meeting so you're able to think on your feet. You'll be pleasantly surprised to find that when you apply the right approach with the right customers, the resulting rapport will make engagement a whole lot smoother.

Chapter 4

Engage

Once the formalities of personal introductions, the exchange of name cards, and small talk have been completed, it's likely that either you or your customer will say, "So let's get down to business, shall we?"

This is the engagement stage where a classic mistake is launching into a monologue about our mighty company and why the customer needs us. Another is apologizing for having interrupted their busy schedule. Yet another is telling them that we'll only take ten minutes. Never short-sell yourself by assuming you know what your customer is feeling.

One security you have is that if you've done the previous stages sufficiently well, you're likely to see a customer who is at ease and ready to listen.

At this stage, you need to present yourself as a genuine expert in your field, but don't get carried away. During your meeting, try to move seamlessly from the established rapport into a two-way-communication arena.

Why did the customer agree to see you? What can you do and say so that he will allow you a second meeting for further exploration? Be cognizant of the fact that from your customer's viewpoint, standard presentations and intrusive questions may not be the ideal way to kick-start the meeting. Hence, when it comes to labeling meetings, I prefer to use the word *engagement* because this carries connotations of being interested, attuned, and attentive during the discussion. Wouldn't it be ideal to have your customer seated upright with all his attention focused on you?

Every question asked by you opens up doors to hidden needs and directs you closer to new possibilities of working together. Visualize every first encounter with a new prospect as if the client is unfailingly receptive and agreeable. Imagine him candidly sharing information you never thought he would reveal.

Give Customers What *They* Want, Not What *We* Want to Give Them

If you go the other way and deliver a lengthy monologue (coupled with your almighty PowerPoint slide presentation) about why the prospective customer needs your solution, *you* could be the reason for his disengaged look. Too often, sales professionals present their solutions to customers without fully understanding their customer's issues and needs. This is because most of us simply can't wait to jump in and talk about *our* company, *our* offering, and how much current customers like *us*.

Jeremiah, a seasoned sales professional of fifteen years in the automotive industry, shared his challenge when dealing with his new Gen-Y customers. He said that, previously, he would simply perform a standard presentation, share a success story, and thereby get the customer to share his requirements. Now however, his Gen-Y customers are unimpressed by success stories. Jeremiah feels that he has to work far harder these days as they are disinterested in how a certain solution has worked for others. Instead, they are interested only in knowing how this solution can be personalized to work for *them*. Does that mean customers are getting more difficult? Well, yes and no. You see, your customers are under intense pressure to perform, beat the competition, and stay ahead of the game. The last thing they need is to have you regurgitate something they already know.

Cook Versus Chef

I once had the opportunity to be invited by a client to a five-star Michelin restaurant in Paris. It was a special menu, even boasting an impressively considered wine-pairing. It was truly a meal for the senses, in which dishes came in a myriad of tempting colors and were even decorated with edible flowers!

There was one particular dessert that stood out—a luscious cake that tasted like a combination of pineapple Jell-O, Oreo cookies, maple syrup, and mint. Despite having an insatiable sweet tooth myself, I found that dessert almost cloyingly sweet.

We both agreed that someone in the kitchen probably *had* been a little over enthusiastic with the maple syrup, and I waved my hand to the head waiter. Almost immediately, my client stopped me, saying, "Reg, maybe we don't know how to appreciate the dessert?"

Having had this seed of doubt planted in my head, I lowered my hand and paused to think. Maybe it was true. How could a five-star Michelin chef make the simple mistake of overdosing on the syrup? After all, he *is* the chef. Would my later reaction have been different if I had purchased the cake from a neighborhood coffee shop? Even if the staff had explained that the cake was prepared with care using only the finest ingredients, I probably would have asked for a refund or demanded another cake instead. Why? The guy who baked that cake was probably a cook who followed a recipe straight from a book and not a gastronomic expert like the chef of a five-star restaurant.

Here, then, is the subtle but significant difference between being seen as a chef or a cook. While a cook is someone who simply prepares the dishes that the customer orders; the chef has credentials. He understands the nuances of customers' taste buds and customizes a menu to suit their palates. His views are sought after as he is truly in tune with the trends and taste of the market. A chef is a trusted advisor, one who truly understands what his customers demand of him. Unafraid of criticism and blunt feedback, he uses his knowledge and the needs of the customers to customize and create a dish that will delight his customers' taste buds. A stellar example of a globally reputed chef would be Gordon Ramsay—one of Britain's highest-profile chefs. He is one of only three chefs in the entire country to maintain three Michelin stars for his restaurant. In spite of the caustic comments he liberally dispenses in his reality TV show *Hell's Kitchen*, he remains highly respected and loved by his peers and loyal customers alike.

To be the level of inspired chef to your customer, you have to initiate rapport and make the customer trust you. You will *not*, however, achieve that by behaving like a talking brochure and only telling them about your company and products.

If you don't make your engagement meaningful to them, you'll be viewed as a cook and be treated like one. In the upcoming section, therefore, we'll discuss how to engage with a customer during the first encounter. What kind of sales professional do you want to be remembered for? plain old cook or ingenious chef?

Engagement—the *E* in FIREFLY

Before engaging the customer, you have to come prepared to impress the customer with your extensive knowledge of his business. There are no shortcuts to forming a positive image.

If you've sized up your customer and *flexed* accordingly, he is probably relaxed by now and ready to find out more. You're on a roll as you've built an setting for you to not only share but also have your customers share with you about *their* needs.

Your goal is to do whatever it takes to engage your customer. This equates to you making an intentional approach to create a two-way conversation. As with building rapport, to create dialogue, the customer must find the topics of relevance to him. To create relevance, you've got to uncover his needs and wants before presenting your solution.

Usually, the first meeting will begin with your company's credential presentation. While it may be viewed as a routine formality, this presentation, if pitched correctly, will resonate deeply with the customer if you can link it to *their* issues.

Probing Comes Before Pitching

Jeremiah, the veteran sales professional, overcame his challenge with the Gen-Y customers by adopting the personal mantra "Don't assume. Ask." Jeremiah soon reaped the gains of implementing this mantra. He observed how much easier it is to maneuver the conversation once he has a bearing about the direction of the conversation and how it helps to prepare questions that soften the ground. By garnering some information about the customer's needs, he now adapts his approach to presenting his company's credentials. Interestingly, Jeremiah has retained the use of standard company slides in his presentations. The difference is that now he knows what to focus on and which areas to emphasize in order to pitch his message more effectively than before.

Now, in comparison to the previous disengaged glazed looks, he is rewarded with engaged nods and questions after his presentation. Instead of a one-way-traffic conversation in which only one party is talking, it has now become a two-way dialogue. Most importantly, customers are now sharing their needs with him openly. They are keen to call him back and curious to find out how he can solve their problems. Jeremiah has finally learned how to engage his customers.

This change in Jeremiah's style was a humbling act for a man who was probably twice the age of his customers today, and yet it was an act that paid off. We obviously need to uncover the customer's needs before making any kind of recommendation. We'll call this sharing of information the needs dialogue. But how does one start this needs dialogue without sounding too authoritative? How do you make the customer comfortable with your process of unearthing what he wants?

Unless you can fully engage and keep the customer's mind-set positive and receptive, your ability to unearth his needs may be limited. It is thus crucial to prepare a dialogue that will be interesting for the customer.

That dialogue is yours to build. You need to build a dialogue in which there is not only (1) sharing of information, but also (2) a two-way engagement to reassure the customer that you are following and empathizing with his train of thought. At the end of the probing conversation, it should be a win not just for you but for both you and the customer. He must walk out of the room feeling that the time he spent with you was thoroughly worthwhile. He should be eagerly anticipating whatever you propose in the next meeting.

OPAL—Engaging with a Question-Based Dialogue

Opals are famed for a multifaceted beauty created by myriad colors coming together with light flawlessly to create the radiant effect that these gemstones possess. Similarly, OPAL engagement is a systematic way of creating a conversation that seamlessly connects the customer's needs to your presentation. It's an approach that provides a structured way to glide into the real issues without appearing too direct and blunt.

In the same way a chef is confident of his knowledge and skill, an OPAL user is has the ability to mingle with his guests with ease. Before making any recommendations, he asks about their preferences and listens intently. He then answers questions from his curious guests and gently suggests several possibilities.

O in OPAL—Opener: Begin with the End in Mind

Start by thanking the customer for his time. However, *never* apologize for interrupting his busy schedule. You are worth his time, not a waste of it. Remember to assume a symmetrical posture, establishing eye contact and a steady pace of voice in order to exude an aura of ease and confidence.

In the opener, be sure to set up the meeting in such a way that it contains two elements:

1. Setting the agenda
2. Testing the waters

- **Agenda**

Let's begin with agenda setting.

Your agenda will affect the mood of the entire meeting. The purpose of designing the agenda is to incorporate a subtle way to identify the initial needs of the customer before diving straight into the "How we can help?" solution.

Break up your credential presentation into three parts.

Part 1: Your Company's Profile

This segment covers your company's profile, history, track record of achievements, and satisfied customer base. The purpose of this is to satisfy the customer's need to know that your company can be relied on.

Part 2: Your Customer's Profile

Tucked between the sections one and two is "understanding his priorities." Explain to the client that you would like to know more about the customer's business before proceeding to part 2 of the credential presentation. The more the customer shares with you, the more effectively you can pitch your company's offering. Consider this section an opportunity for you to gently uncover both the stated *and* hidden needs of the customer.

Part 3: Your Company's Offer

Once you get a perspective on the customer's views, you'll be better prepared to frame your corporate presentation to focus on areas he is keen on. In this way—even if you are still using standard presentation slides—you'll be ready to zoom in on areas from the feedback you received in part 2.

While walking through the agenda, keep the customer engaged by asking him if there is anything in particular that he would like you to cover. After you arrive at an agreed agenda, you can proceed to part 1 of your corporate presentation.

- **Testing the waters**

Before starting, it's a good idea to test the waters before jumping into the deep end of your presentation. Before addressing a specific subject, it's advisable to get a glimpse of the customer's view on it. Below are a couple of techniques I've found to be helpful.

Technique #1: Did You Know?

One way is to test the waters is to use the "Did you know?" question to evoke a response. For example, if you want to share a story about your involvement in the lighting services for the recent Formula One night race, you could test the waters by asking, "Did you know that fifty-seven thousand light bulbs were used during the recent Formula One race?"

If the customer were to respond with a question like "Oh, really? That's a staggering number of bulbs!" you could reply with an affirmative "Indeed, it was interesting, really, because we were one of the vendors for that project." His response gives you an idea of his interest in that subject matter.

Conversely, if the customer were to reply with a "No, but I'm not a fan so I wouldn't know," or "Yes, but those lights are different from ours," then you have a hint that this might not be the right way to go. It's probably timely that you change the topic instead.

Technique #2: What Is Your Opinion?

Another way to test the waters is to ask his opinion on a subject matter by asking an open-ended question like "What is your opinion?"

Using the same Formula One race example, you can ask, "What's your opinion on the recent newspaper article on the energy-friendly lights used during the recent night race?" Depending on his level of interest and enthusiasm, you can gather enough information to know if that topic is worth pursuing.

Planting your question during your opener allows you to test the waters, without committing yourself to a course of action, to see if the topic is of value or interest to the customer. With the feedback you get, you'll be better prepared and less likely to encounter any unexpected nasty comments.

In summary, work on your agenda and opening questions before beginning your meeting so you can hit the ground running once you begin your presentation.

P in OPAL—Probe: Engagement Is Not a Guessing Game!

At this stage, I am assuming you have done the initial corporate presentation and have a fair understanding of the customer's profile and needs.

Make It Easy for the Customer

Stay flexible during the meeting so you can seize the opportunity to ask relevant questions. Remember that most times, it's not *what* you ask but *how* you ask it. Plan your questions well so that you can get the answers you need to pitch your offering correctly.

Tailor your questions so it doesn't sound to the customer that you are dishing out standard checklist questions—the surest way to make your customer disengage! Organize and keep your questions simple and noncontroversial. The last thing you want to do is to put your customer in a spot or embarrass him. Make the effort to offer constructive ideas as you gather information from the customer. No one appreciates talking to an inert sponge.

Avoid asking close-ended questions as it appears interrogative and limits the answers the customer can provide. Instead, ask open-ended questions, and be polite in how you phrase them. Whenever possible, try to give a viewpoint or statement before asking a question so that you appear credible and knowledgeable.

Differentiating between Needs and Wants

We ask questions because we want to know what the customer needs so that we can close that gap by meeting that need. However, over the course of my professional journey, I've received numerous questions about the difference between a need and a want. Here's my answer:

Needs are based on function. Typically, you'll hear customers begin by saying, "I want the best and the cheapest!" Since that equation is not realistic, your job is to clarify what he means by *best* and how he arrived at the inference of *cheapest*.

With probing, you'll begin to uncover the hidden concerns behind the stated needs. Most times, customers want more than their basic needs met.

Wants are different from *needs* and connote something that goes beyond a rational need. Examples of wants (i.e., higher-level needs) are the need to be seen as a crafty negotiator, the need to be number 1 in the marketplace, or the need to mitigate risk and prevent unnecessary problems.

What You Ask Is What You Get

The answers to your questions must satisfy the following:

- Do I understand the customer's business and their challenges?
- Do I have a solution that can address the gap described by the customer?

Because every prospect is unique, the probing approach needs to be reviewed and organized. While most of the questions are similar, the manner in which you prioritize and word them must be adaptable.

Here are seven questions to help you qualify the prospective customer and confirm that you are able to provide a solution to address his needs. All these answers will form a tapestry of inputs and enable you to decide if the customer is worth pursuing.

I've come up with an apt mnemonic to make it easier for you to recall the seven questions. All you need to remember is THREAD$. Note, however, that THREAD$ is a general model. The questions should be adapted to the market that you operate in and refined even further to accommodate the specific customer you are planning to meet.

Avoid generic questions as far as possible. You want to ensure that you can ask contextualized *relevant* questions so that the customer becomes *impressed* by your questioning approach.

Seven Questions with THREAD$ through the Qualification Process

T: Time line—What is the time line to complete the project?
H: Heightened needs—What are the needs and wants related to the intended goal?
R: Rank—What are his priorities with respect to the challenges raised?
E: Evaluation—What are his criterions for evaluation of the vendor selection?
A: Application—How will he be using the solution(s) to meet the priorities?
D: Decision making—What are the decision-making processes and staff dynamics like?
$: Budget—What is his budget range?

Working with these questions will help you gain a clearer insight into the potential opportunity of the customer. Keep in mind that the customer may choose not to reveal too much in the early stages, so it is imperative to ensure that (with the help of THREAD$) you know which questions you need to ask in order to garner information.

Distill Your Questions with 7-5-3 Shuffle

If you ever need to organize your questions, try the 7-5-3 shuffle technique. This is a technique to help your prioritize your questions during the conversation. By consciously arranging your questions, you will be able to start the meeting with the right question.

The composition of the right set of questions will depend largely on how you feel the questions will sit with the customer. If your first question is an intrusive one, such as "You did not make a profit in the last quarter. What do you think was the reason for that?" it should be no surprise if the customer reacts unfavorably. Here are the steps you should take to ensure a comfortable questioning process:

1. Set the objectives of your questions. This way you'll know how so that you can prioritize the questions in later steps.
2. Brainstorm and come up with seven questions (we've chosen the magic number 7 to allow you to cover enough ground while still remaining crisp and concise). There is no need to prioritize the questions.
3. Review the seven questions. Downgrade two of them by comparing their importance to the objectives you set in step 1. Re-rank the selected questions to number 7 (least important) and number 6. You should now be left with five unranked questions.
4. Review the remaining five questions. Downgrade two more questions by validating their quality to your step 1 objectives. Re-rank those two questions as numbers 5 and 4. You are now left with three questions.
5. Review the three questions and force-rank each question.
6. Your questions are now ready and prioritized from number 1 through 7.
7. Review the prioritized questions, and test the questions with a colleague to see if it's worded well. Rephrase them until you are satisfied.

Congratulations! You've just completed your 7-5-3 shuffle, and you're set to uncover your customer's needs. Having organized and prioritized your questions, you'll feel more comfortable in probing for information and be better able to focus your approach. If you're strapped for time or faced with an impatient customer, you'll also have the tools you need to think on your feet and lead the dialogue without hesitating.

Most importantly, you'll make the customer so comfortable with you that he may even volunteer more information to help you sharpen your proposal. Impressing the customer with your line of questioning will sculpt his perception of you into that of a master chef, rather than a recipe-following cook. Voilà!

The Customer Will Respond to Your Questions. Be Sensitive.

Meanwhile, remember that asking questions requires tact and grace. Phrasing your questions so they are palatable will promote openness with the prospect. If he appears distracted, fidgets, or resists answering your question, don't insist on more details.

If the customer demonstrates signs of awkwardness or shyness, redirect the conversation to him and ask if there are questions that he would like to ask you instead. In this way, you give him the chance to lead the dialogue.

On the other hand, if the customer is tight-lipped and replies to a question with ambivalent responses like "maybe" or "it depends," it may mean your question is too broad. Rephrase your question in more specific terms and probe gently.

Sometimes providing multiple-choice options can also help the customer warm up at the start of the engagement. Cite examples from customer feedback or common market practices for him to comment on. Avoid close-ended questions at all times.

Once you've tried the 7-5-3 shuffle technique, you'll realize the value of relevant, well-thought-out questions. Clarifying questions can help the customer distill his thoughts too. Sometimes it just takes a series of poignant yet relevant questions to help someone sort out his thoughts and gain insights.

Probing dialogue can also be a powerful avenue for you to demonstrate your credibility and grasp of your customer's market. Customers do appreciate sales professionals who come prepared and eager to add value even from the first meeting. In sum, don't compromise and skip your homework before the first meeting. The quality of the subsequent probing dialogues will determine your relevance to the customer.

A in OPAL—Align: Show Your Customer that You Understand

Even with good-probing dialogue, you still have to engage the customer so it doesn't become a one-way conversation. Can you imagine how a customer will feel if, after having shared earnestly for twenty minutes about the demanding internal pressures in his organization, he is met with a perfunctory response by you like "Thanks, I'll provide a proposal in a week's time?"

If you have been guilty of doing that up till now, stop that habit this minute. Instead, seize the chance to impress and connect with your customer even more. Show him that you understand what he said. Show him that he has not wasted his time talking to a wallflower.

As he talks to you, go beyond writing down your notes but maintain eye contact with occasional nodding to show your attentiveness. Summarize or probe further to show your understanding and personal interest of his plight.

How does one align with the customer? In your mind, combine his responses to each separate question and piece together a coherent picture of the customer's requirements.

Some may mistake that as impromptu speaking. On the contrary, aligning with another person's world happens when you can mirror his feeling and thoughts by expounding on ideas, insights, and stories that he has shared.

Aligning will earn your credibility with the customer. This is because he hears what you're saying and that tells him that you have understood him well. By now, the customer would feel at ease with you and now you have earned the right to dive deeper into the conversation.

Align with Show-and-Tell

Aligning comes in two parts: showing and telling. Experienced sales professionals use this structured approach unconsciously, but it's easy to master once you internalize it.

Show the Customer You Understand His CORE Needs

Showing is all about connecting to the flow of information and showing your customer you understand his core needs. The process by which this is achieved is called CORE. To begin, summarize your thoughts using CORE as follows:

C—Context: The setting is defined by the customer's business model, the solutions they offer, and the circumstances relevant to their operations.
>Example: "I understand that you're in the business of customizing upholstery materials for commercial manufacturers. I also understand that current business margins are fast eroding due to cutthroat prices pushed by competition from Asia despite being of lesser quality."

O—Opportunity: The possibility that we could create a favorable outcome despite current challenges.
>Example: "If your customers are able to differentiate between the benefits of your high-quality material and the risks associated with your competitors' inferior material, your customers will be more inclined to make decisions in your favor."

R—Results: The outcome(s) desired as defined by the customer.
>Example: "You're looking for a marketing campaign that will improve the conversion rate of sales proposals to sampling by 20 percent annually."

E—Expectation: The desired standards as defined by the customer such as service level, expertise, and other benchmarks specified in the evaluation criteria of a vendor.
>Example: "You've mentioned that apart from completing the project on time, the vendor must be able to provide more value-added services. These include providing promotional ideas during a campaign

design and having web analytics to adequately analyze the campaign's performance."

Depending on the conversation flow, CORE can be used in different ways. You can align back to show your understanding at appropriate junctures, or you can use CORE as a summary at the end of the exploratory probing session.

Align and Tell Your Customer How You Can Help

The *telling* part of show-and-tell is last but not least. As it may be too early for you to develop a recommendation during that discussion, you can keep your customer interested by sharing a related success story instead. Tell him how your solution has helped another customer, then tell him that your solution for *his* problems will be relevant and contextual to his needs.

Why tell him a success story? When you tell him a success story, you're stimulating his interest and infusing trust. Proof of your previous successes will not only plant the expectations of future success but will also reassure him that you are not a greenhorn by demonstrating related experiences. Further, by telling him a success story, you will gain leverage via third-party endorsement. The success story you share should be concise yet compelling enough to leave him wanting to find out more.

How to share a success story?

Use the CARD tool to make your customer sit up and listen when you show him how you have helped other customers in similar situations. Here is an example of how you can apply CARD to tell your success story

Storytelling with CARD

C—Challenge: Client X was in a situation similar to the one your present client is in. Client X had experienced severe price erosion with several new competitors.
A—Action: We launched a campaign that provided a thirty-day money-back guarantee. We concurrently ran a rebate program with his loyal customer base.

R—Results: In three months, Client X's customers saw a 40 percent improvement in trial rates. At the end of six months, we reversed the two-year-price erosion with a price increase of 7 percent.

D—Differentiation: The difference in our approach to Client X's potential competitors was our strong analytics in tracking the campaign. By tracking the campaign closely, we could adjust our marketing mechanics according to weekly results.

Using a simple yet compelling story like this, you have yet another way to align to your customer's needs by sharing how you have helped *a* previous customer. Your customer can now relate to what you can do for them.

So far you've seen how important it is to stay connected to the customer's world by reaching out in a manner that is aligned to his world view.

_L_ in OPAL—Link: Summarize and Reflect Back What was Discussed

The final element in OPAL addresses how essential it is for you to end the conversation on a positive note in order to create a positive impression on the customer.

When you have completed the probing session and other items on the agenda, you have an opportunity to connect back to the intended agenda. The conversation has probably covered a range of topics and so it is time for you need to consolidate.

Summarizing the Agenda Points

Summarize the key areas that have been covered and proceed to ask the customer if he needs any clarification about your offering. If you have any collateral to leave behind, provide a quick overview.

Checking for Clarification

You may need a follow-up email or call after reviewing the minutes of the meeting. Be proactive and check with the client his preferred mode of communication and the best hours of the day to contact him.

Suspending Judgment

Sometimes dealing with difficult customers can be emotionally draining for you, and naturally, your opinion about the customer or the business potential may be clouded. It's difficult, but try your best to suspend judgment and stay objective. When you consciously do that, you'll become less affected by your emotions and can focus better on the facts. Set aside your prejudices and opinions, and remind yourself that you are present to learn what the customer has to say, not the other way around.

Finally, thank your prospect for taking the time to share his honest feedback and opinions with you, and summarize your next action to affirm your proactive follow through.

In spite of all the convenience of high-tech communication with e-mails and SMS, it is still nice to use the traditional snail-mail approach after calling on the customer. Send a thank-you letter or card as a personal touch to show your appreciation for his time.

Your ability to build trust and credibility happens at the first meeting. While it's hard work and requires time to prepare, doing so will go a long way toward getting the right information you need.

Summary

Getting a customer to share his needs with you can be challenging if you don't lead the conversation well. If you want to be perceived as a chef and not a cook, you've got to take charge of the conversation with a proactive and systematic probing dialogue.

Customers who are participative and involved during the probing dialogue may share and open more to you if you use the OPAL tools. Start with the right questions and test the waters before diving in. Plan your questions with THREAD$ so you can qualify your customers with the right questions.

Stay aligned with the customer by doing your show-and-tell so that the customer feels assured of your understanding and confident of your ability to deliver on your promises. Suspend your own judgment during the needs dialogue and stay focused on the customer.

Finally, conclude the conversation by linking to the agenda and doing one final clarification for both sides.

Chapter 5

Flow

This is the moment of truth: the presentation of your company's solution.

Depending on the complexity of your business, this may take a twenty-minute presentation or several visits.

After you've completed the *FIRE* in FIREFLY, you should know enough about your prospect's business and professional and personal needs by now to size up their requirements. If you don't feel confident in doing so, revisit the FIRE phase. It's important to reverse gears before you present your pitch.

As a consultative expert, I have come to realize that if you fail to establish rapport and build common ground during the early stages of relationship building, you'll find it challenging to fully grasp the needs of the customer in the later stage. Before you jump on the presentation bandwagon, review your engagement to ensure you have probed enough to uncover your customer's needs and priorities and to ensure that your solution has adequately addressed them.

This Is Not an Elevator Speech

Your final presentation is the defining twist to the engagement phase. Many people mistake their presentation as the final opportunity to sell their products and services to the customer and embark on an overzealous hard-sell approach that covers every facet of how perfect their solutions are for the customer. When they get rejected by the customer, they get stomped and wondered which part of their proposal the customer failed to understand.

Well, here's the thing: Today's customer is more sophisticated, savvier, and discerning. They may not have given in to the pomp and pizzazz of your sleek presentation. Yes, your presentation might be comprehensive, but bear in mind that today's customer is inundated with information and distraction of this kind. With information overload, he is seeking a vendor who can be trusted to delivery on the right solution for his need.

Gordon, a strategic executive whose job is to select vendors for collaborative projects, finds that most presentations inflate the value of their offering. They proclaim the relative superiority of their solution to the competition but inevitably lack a crystal-clear definition of the benefit from the customer's perspective

FLOW—the *F* in FIREFLY

This section is entitled "Flow", and is the segment of the FIREFLY tool used to present your solution. Now we will examine *why* exactly we have titled this segment "Flow." One definition of *flow* is "to derive from a source." This reminds us that the ultimate aim of the presentation should be centered on the *source* of the flow—the needs of the customer.

The other meaning of *flow* is an active verb meaning "smooth continuity." That's the kind of energy we want to create in our presentation—not a unidirectional pitch. How do we create this flow? Certainly not by using a standard presentation kit and expecting the customer to fit your approach!

Connect Seamlessly with Your Customer's World

Customers see lots of presentations and are quick to identify quick fixes and instant pitches from vendors. If you want to stand out from the crowd, you've got to do more than merely point out relevant slides from your standard presentation kit.

Do the thinking for the customer and spare him the pain. In the solutions presentation, you don't just want to pick a ready-made solution from your sales kit. Instead, create a smooth-flowing recommendation centered on the customer's world and his particular problem.

Why? Because you're intentionally focused on his perspective and approaching the solutions presentation from his viewpoint. It's important that you design presentations that flow from the customer's viewpoint so you can enable him to seamlessly glide from one slide to the next.

When you flow in your conversation, your customers will relate better to you.

How to Flow with Your Solution: Don't sell—*Solve*!

When you prepare your presentation to a customer, it's normal to want to stand out from the competitors; and indeed, you should aim for this! You want to impress upon the customer that you know what the best solution is and why you are the best person to work with them.

Patricia, a twenty-eight-year-old rookie in the game of selling industrial materials, faced a challenge in the price-sensitive hard-hat market. Many of her colleagues—most of them twice her age—told her that she would sell well because of her pretty face. I remember Patricia well because she hired me as an executive coach to help her prove to her peers that she was *more* than just a pretty face. With consultation sessions, we came up with a plan to help her prove that she was on top of her game.

First, Patricia made it a point to get to know more people by being present at the site and engage with the on-site supervisors. Then she set out to learn more about the application of building materials relative to the market trend, architect's preference, and current construction costs. In other words, instead of simply placing emphasis on price discounts, she was able to discuss the need for marketability and quality, drawing the customer's attention to the fact that these two traits were of paramount importance to a successful building project.

Despite the fact that Patricia's customers were not used to her non-price approach at the beginning, they were soon won over by her ability to relate to the demands of the developers' expectations.

When I caught up with Patricia recently, she told me that things had been easier since converting to the flow approach in her presentation, with her customers being impressed by her depth of knowledge despite her youth. To her, that compliment was better than getting a pay raise!

Patricia focused on the outcomes for the customers and extended that view beyond the usual price discounting call. Was it an easy pitch? "Never, and you don't get the instant dotted-line signature either," quipped Patricia, recently promoted to regional sales representative. "However, the customer never says no either. Instead, by evoking his curiosity with my non-price approach, we would have an open dialogue about his views so that I could understand both he and his needs better. My closing rates have been so much better since."

Patricia took the effort to relate her business solution to her customer's perspective. Contextualizing her solution using the construction background of the customer, she tailored her solution to their operational and marketing approach.

If you have engaged the customer sufficiently during the rapport and engagement stage, you will be able to do the same thing as Patricia. You will have a total picture of his business, context, and expectations. What you should do from there is continue to align to your customer's world based on the picture you have formed.

If you want to flow, the general one-size-fits-all brochures or PowerPoint will need more than just a cosmetic facelift. If you're faced with savvy corporate customers and/or buyers with strong purchasing muscles, you'll need to exercise greater judgment in identifying your primary value to that company.

By tailoring your solution to *their* needs, you'll raise your value to the prospect. The prospect will be interested in what you have to say because it gives them a direct, personalized solution to what *they* were worrying about.

Patricia's customized approach to her sales presentation did not come intuitively. She had failed several times, and when we spoke, she remarked that she had problems learning her products and price list by heart. So when I told her to ditch that approach and use the flow approach instead, she accepted the challenge with a gung ho attitude. She is now doing very well and her dialogues with her customers are less focused on price too.

Stop Self-Destructive Time Bombs

Here are some quick fixes for common mistakes that can instantly hurt the credibility of your presentation and destroy your customer's attention span in a snap. These top five mistakes can kill the flow in any presentation:

1. *No more business buzzwords.* What this means is that you'll have to stop using tacky business buzzwords such as "best-of-breed solutions," "best value for money," and "world-class quality." These non-contextual phrases mean nothing to the customer.
2. *No more irrelevant sales pitches.* Forget about all your product features and performance. Instead, with your research, relate your solutions to *their* industry and business context. Stay relevant to the audience's needs and expectations.
3. *No more parroting a selling monologue.* Selling is not just about talk. It is about structuring your presentation in a way that will excite the customer and make him curious to learn more about your solution. Stay concise and create an interactive dialogue.
4. *No more excesses.* Too much of anything is never good. Refrain from indulging in too many slides, props, or details. Instead, balance your presentation such that your message is conveyed clearly without getting too cluttered.
5. *No more fluff without evidence.* Once you've got the solution out, be ready to do your show-and-tell to convince them with evidence and success stories. Don't weaken your customer's perception of your solution by a lack of facts.

The Work Starts before the Presentation

Although flowing with your customer's business and expectations will take extra work and additional clarification, rest assured that, like Patricia, you will see the payoff. Ultimately, customers respond well to enthusiastic and politely persistent sales professionals.

Will I irritate the customer if I return with more questions, you ask? Not if you approach them with positive energy and a refreshing desire to help them solve their problems. When you ask constructive questions, you build more trust with your customers because they will be impressed by your energy and determination to design a solution for them. They will open up to you slowly and surely.

Seek Out the Invisible Forces

If you've done sufficient probing during the engagement stage, you'll have some idea of the customer's decision-making dynamics.

Process: Find out how the process of decision making is done and who is in the decision-making team. That will give you an estimation of the duration of time the engagement will take.

People: Get to know as many people as possible during the engagement process. If you have a team working together, review comments from different departments to see how you can integrate and balance diverse needs and opinions.

Problems: Don't be quick to assume that you clearly understand what the problem is. Instead, take the time to drill down to find challenges and problems with the customer in order to fully understand the details.

Personal agenda: Everyone always has a personal agenda and customers are no exception. Get to know these personal motives. Is this project your customer's ticket to a big promotion? Is there friction between the two heads of department? Keep you antenna up and sieve out emotional or hidden needs. Your customer's personal agenda is just as important as his business needs.

Perception: Be mindful of things valued as sacred cows and be discerning before attempting to challenge the status quo or long held beliefs of the company. Check out your customer's past experiences, especially areas where there were unfavorable outcomes or bad press. The last thing you want is to face a brick wall because your recommendation is incongruous with their current views and values.

Stay Conscious of Your Nonverbal Signals

As a presenter, watch your body language to ensure that you don't accidentally give off the wrong signals. We all know how unnerving it can be presenting to a large group or an intimidating individual, so brace yourself and practice, practice, practice.

When you present, you want customers to feel that you're flowing with them and are comfortable with the content you're presenting. There should be no element of doubt or fear; instead you should be seen to be exuding confidence with the right posture.

When you are conscious of your nonverbal gestures, you'll create harmony because your body gestures will be in tandem with what you are saying, and you'll create a positive impact—definitely the message you want to convey.

If you're standing, stay symmetrical in your posture and avoid swaying or fidgeting. Leave your hands clasped gently in front of you or let them relax at your sides. Hold your chin up and face the audience. If you have a large audience, scan the room in a random Z formation so it seems as if you're making eye contact with everyone.

Nobody likes a wooden character with over rehearsed gestures. Make the effort to be natural and spontaneous with your gestures. Be careful not to go overboard with excessive or repetitive movements as this gets distracting for the audience. Finally, never use your index finger to emphasize your point as it may appear rude or aggressive.

Get the Basics Right from the Beginning

Unless you demonstrate confidence and exude a professional enthusiasm, the presentation will be incomplete. Customers always buy you before they buy the solution, which means you've got to project credible charisma from the inside out.

Engaging the customer in the presentation may seem hard, but even when you're presenting you need to build trust and establish your credibility as the trusted advisor.

You've probably heard the following three sentences before, but they bear repeating. Though simplistic, they offer great advice and work well as a personal mantra during presentations.

The mantra is as follows:

- Tell your audience what you're going to tell them.
- Tell them.
- Then tell them what you told them.

This principle will make your audience comfortable and secure because they'll know where you're headed. With this clarity, you will motivate yourself to get the right information and frame the presentation according to what is important to them. Most importantly, this mantra will motivate you to go the extra mile so that you can achieve the ultimate goal: satisfy and exceed your customers' needs.

Stand Out from the Competition

Contrary to the conventional approach to starting a presentation with your accolades, chances are that yours are no different from your competition. So how do you stand out from the competition? By keeping your presentation clear, crisp, and compelling. Design a seamless yet interesting flow so that the customer follows your sequence and logic without hesitation.

What's the key to a powerful and commanding presentation?

Flow—Stand Out with GPS, and Keep Them Begging for More

To make your presentation flow, you need to lead, communicate, and build up momentum as you share what you can do for them. There are three steps in your solutions presentation, whether it's a formal boardroom meeting or a casual recommendation. It's called the GPS model.

The global positioning system, or GPS, is a technical marvel created by deploying satellites to transmit accurate location, speed, and time information. Your current position can be tracked live wherever you are.

Like its technical counterpart, the GPS model allows you to flow your presentation with an accurate pitch by staying focused on what is important to the customer. Using GPS, you can discard irrelevant information and design a pitch that connects to the heart of the customer. This will empower you to create a solution the customer will appreciate.

Mix and Mingle with the Audience

The GPS approach focuses on making your presentation relevant and meaningful, not only to a general corporate company, but to each individual at the meeting. Timeliness of information provides an immediate connection to the person in front of you.

Keep yourself engaged and at the forefront the moment you set foot into the meeting room. Once you've finished setting up, mix and mingle with the audience. Work the room with a self-introduction and name-card exchange. Break the ice with everyone wherever possible so you don't end up presenting to a room full of strangers. Don't let their seniority get in the way—be confident and allow your enthusiasm and energy to infuse the room. Your aim is to create a warm and professional atmosphere.

While making small talk, take the opportunity to ask about their views and opinions on issues that might be relevant for your presentation. Make use of both casual and credible rapport to warm up the introductions. Gather information and remember names so that you can use them to instill a sense of familiarity during the presentation.

Mike, a young presenter I ran into recently, is an excellent retainer of information each time he does a presentation. With his strong relational skills, he mingles with and then remembers the names of the people he met. Without putting anyone on the spot, he makes use of the introduction session to seamlessly weave comments into his presentation to make it relevant to his target audience. He uses facts and feelings gathered during the mingling period to engage and immediately flow with his audience.

Let's walk through the GPS approach and see how you can freshen your presentation, connect with the audience, and create a smooth flow by connecting to the customer's needs.

G—Grabber

The way you start your opening will set the tone for the rest of the session. If you can capture your audience's attention, warm it up, and establish rapport, it reduces the stress and anxiety of the entire presentation. Begin with enthusiasm, and inject a little personality into your opening. Whenever possible, relate aspects of the valuable information you just gathered to specific points in your presentation.

After greeting the audience, scan the room and introduce your team mates if it's a team effort. Never apologize or belittle yourself when doing self introduction.

While remaining warm and engaging, be discerning about the use of humor. While successful humor can inject a great element into your opening; humor is subjective and should be used only if you know with certainty that the target audience will respond positively. Obviously, a room full of undertakers will respond differently to gallows humor than will a room full of parents. Storytelling can be a powerful opening tool too—start with a fable or even a customer testimonial, and your audience will listen to every word and visualize the verbal imagery you project. Paint a picture; and either complete the story with a link to your objectives or leave it as a cliff-hanger. If you do leave a cliff-hanger, don't forget to complete your story at the end of your presentation!

Other ways that you can grab attention with your opening include the following:

- A interesting quotation
- A market report or research finding
- A question or riddle
- A desired outcome or future state

Just remember that how you open will stir a specific emotion and create an immediate impression with your audience. That means investing in the basics and getting it right from the get-go.

P—Present

Use the **COPPER** technique to present. Your pitch must position you as a good conductor of success—just like copper, which is a good conductor of electricity. In this case, the acronym COPPER stands for current state, opportunity, problems, proposition, execution, and reinforce.

You organize the presentation based on how you want the customer to respond, not what you want to accomplish. As such, to create a persuasive presentation, step aside from the organization that you represent and immerse in the customer's world of worries and challenges.

If you get stuck wondering what to include or omit in the presentation, put yourself in the customer's shoes. Just imagine walking through multiple presentations with different vendors. What would you wish that the vendors did more of and less of?

C—Current State

Describe the current state of your customer's business based on the information you have collected. Consolidate the salient business drivers, competitive arena, and market situation to ensure that your customers agree with your initial summation.

This is also a chance for you to check back with the audience to see if anything has changed since the last meeting. State your assumptions and clarify with the audience before you begin. In this way, you can find out if there have been recent developments, and you will have caught them early and can angle your presentation accordingly.

> Example: "Today's industry is marred by severe price erosion with the entry of foreign players keen to gain quick market share. You have shared that you will never compromise the quality of your service and support or submit to the price wars

as this would be detrimental to the organization's future. Is that synopsis correct?"

O—Opportunity

Describe a favorable or advantageous circumstance based on your customer's current background, which could become a potential future state. Provide possible scenarios, and articulate the benefits that customers would enjoy if they seized the chance to resolve a current obstacle or problem.

> Example: "Despite current global conditions, we believe there are new ways to exploit your current base of loyal customers and significantly develop your market presence outside North America within the next five years."

P—Problems

Describe any current and potential weaknesses, threats, and vulnerabilities to the customer's business in an objective matter without stretching the truth. If you are implying that a latent problem might lead to a negative consequence down the road, provide reasons why you feel that is so. Don't generalize or use hearsay in your explanation.

> Example: "The current challenges you have identified are poor visibility and articulation of the brand's unique strengths. In addition to that, Forbes research indicates that the increasing cost of raw materials is likely to increase your production costs too."

Nor do you have to stick with obvious problems. If you think new problems may crop up as a result of current or trending circumstances, bring them up too.

> Example: "If you invest in above the line advertising campaigns, the lag in response from the market will erode your margins even further. If you choose to reduce your marketing campaign, your customers may switch to other promotional-driven brands. However, at the current rate, if you maintain the status quo, the competitive pressures may erode your market share."

P—Proposition

Now is the time to offer a proposal or a solution that shows how *you* can be the catalyst to help your customer triumph in the future.

Define and support your solution. It's essential to use a logical and linear approach so your customer is able to easily follow your train of thought. If the solution is a complex or a multifaceted combination of sub-elements, then ensure that you present an overarching proposition before you cluster the other elements into sections and subsections. It's important to be sensitive to the customer's ability to capture the essence otherwise, you'll risk having a customer who is lost but embarrassed to ask for clarification. Worse still, you might find yourself facing a micro manager who picks on the little things instead of looking at the bigger picture.

Focus on using a unique value proposition to differentiate your proposal. What is a unique value proposition? It's the unique competency your company offers—something you can do better than any of your competitors. For example, it could be a core competency that you excel in consistently, or it could be a solution that you have more expertise in than anyone else. Unless your customer believes that your value is truly different from the rest *and* can help him achieve his goals, all you are to your customer is another cookie-cutter commodity.

Whenever possible, use the customer's own jargon to align yourself with him. In addition, align your solution to your customer's focus and business model. Use specific and not general statements as the latter will dilute the perceived effectiveness of your proposal.

In public relations (PR), there's something called the message house. It simply means that the PR practitioner chooses a single message rather than a plethora of sub-messages when communicating with a stakeholder. This allows the full structure of the house to support the central idea. Visualize a roof (idea) held up by three pillars—each pillar being justification for the idea. Why three? Clustering your key-support points to a maximum of three vastly improves customers' recall rate.

Adapting that idea here, we can call this the proposition house by simply substituting *proposition* for *idea*.

Example: "Our sales contact management system will provide you with a seamless customer contact plan that enables you to promote the right solutions to the right audience. The success of this system is evident by three supporting points:

1. our integrated marketing and operations facility;
2. our local experts who understand your needs; and
3. the back-end analytics that provide up-to-date information for improved decision making.

Combining these three pillars, we'll integrate all essential operations to ensure that you continuously connect with your customer base through a closed-loop system."

Whether your aim is to inform, persuade, or educate during this proposition stage, make sure you organize and package your message so that it's easy for the customer to receive. You want him to understand you and to easily recall your key points.

E—Execution

Tell your customer how you plan to implement the solution by giving an overview of your intent. When you present your ideas here, keep them crisp and broad, withholding detailed information until asked. At this point, you don't want to get bogged down in side trips into back alleys; you want to present a clear overview. When you share your execution approach, come prepared with extra handouts in the event that more questions are asked.

Be open and receptive to feedback throughout the presentation stage. It would not do you any good to leave all comments until the completion of the pitch. Plan for questions so that you are able to solicit feedback at critical junctures. When you get questions, decide if you are ready to reply or park the question until the completion of the presentation. With every question asked, you are a step nearer to knowing their thoughts, doubts, and uncertainties. A good presentation is not one way but a two-way interactive dialogue that is not intimidating. The dialogue enables you to understand how they have received the message and give the customer an opportunity to air their views too. Keep him coming back for more. Make the customer buy. Don't sell.

Your customers don't want your execution phase to sound like a lecture, so make your approach lively and colorful by speaking in short crisp sentences. Cluster phases into smaller chunks so that your customers are better able to absorb the message.

You might find the following four suggestions useful in streamlining and simplifying your approach:

- *Divide and conquer.* Divide your projects into smaller sections with independent but well-defined goals leading to the overall project goal. An example of this is organizing an event with different activities on the agenda. There are numerous subprojects like ticket sales, advertising, etc., but all working toward an overarching goal.
- *Snowballing.* Start with the infrastructure phase, explaining why the foundation is essential. Then define all the subprojects that will follow thereafter. An example would be starting a customer-relationship software module that requires information from different departments to be integrated into one common platform.
- *Satellite stations.* Organize your execution around large projects called satellites. Sub-projects then revolve around each main satellite project. Unlike snowballing, which focuses on a single platform that meshes all subprojects, the satellite technique is comprised of several foundations that remain independent but are each essential to the completion of the whole project. An example of this is building a mixed commercial and residential property in which each development can operate on an independent time line.
- *Achilles heel.* Define the project based on a critical factor upon which the success of the entire project hinges. This could be the availability of a specific raw material, deadline for completion, or stock availability. With this technique, start by highlighting the crucial make-or-break element in the implementation stage and centering all subsequent activities around it. An example of this technique is launching a phone campaign by first securing all the

primary media bookings and blocking out the competition during the first week of the launch.

R—Reinforce

Besides using the standard features and benefits explanation, generate interest by using different approaches to prove your concept. It will allow your customers to appreciate different facets of your solution. Reinforce this again at the end.

Having established the emotional connection from your persuasive messaging, sealing the finale helps address the rational need of your customer. STEAD consists of five techniques (with examples) you can use to show proof of your concept:

- Statistics: "Customers will see a 25 percent improvement in online orders."
- Testimonial: "Carter Corporation successfully used our solution in Beijing."
- Example: "You can use the software to do targeted promotions."
- Analogy: "Our systems run with a hub-and-spoke approach."
- Demonstration: "This is how easy the user interface is."

Context-based evidence will convince the customer that you are able to deliver on your promise. You will be able to inspire trust because your proofs are shining examples of how your solution has *already* worked so well!

S—Seal

When you conclude your presentation, build a momentum in the final step of the GPS model. Having grabbed their attention and pitched a solution that flowed with the outcomes they wanted, seal the conclusion with a powerful finish.

The last impression you want to give is that you are either desperate or aggressive. Therefore, be conscious of your pace and never rush to close the deal. In your closing message, your customer should be inspired by your enthusiasm and confidence to see him succeed in his business with your solution.

Your summary should aim to strike a chord with the customer by relating back to how your organization provides the ideal solution for their needs.

So seize the opportunity to encourage your audience to review and ask questions to ensure that they have absorbed your key points. Use these questions to confirm if they fully understood what you said and ensure that you create an avenue of consultative dialogue.

If you have also garnered strong support from a particular individual, now is the time to have him comment on your presentation; as long as you're confident, he is an influential individual in the meeting.

This is a platform for you to create a continuous dialogue with your customers and engage their viewpoints. Being prepared for different interpretation and possible dissentions would help you understand your customer's perspectives better.

And hence, you have sealed the presentation in two ways. One, you have presented a compelling solution by placing yourself in their shoes, and secondly, you have garnered their respect when you engage in a fruitful dialogue to engage their views so that you can understand them better.

Summary

The customer must be wowed by your presentation, so don't use a standard approach. Even when the same solution is in play, no two customers are alike, so you need to understand the needs and the decision dynamics before you craft your tailored message.

When you apply the GPS in the way you flow in a presentation, you are simply focused on creating a grabber at the opening, presenting an outcome-based solution in the middle and sealing the conclusion on a high note about your ability by encouraging open dialogue and clarification. When you present, always stay relevant and match your pitch to the customer's needs. Even if the solution is a standard one, try to adapt by using the customer's own language and jargon.

Presenting an outcome-based solution requires you to readjust your perspective. By using the COPPER tool, you'll intentionally wrap your solution around the context of the customer's business.

Nobody can sell fluff anymore. If you want to stay ahead of the crowd, you've got to utilize your knowledge of your customer's business to help you develop the pitch. You've only got one chance, so never take the easy way with a one-size-fits-all solution.

You will stand out from the competition because the customers know that you know what they want. Your knowledge of them will gain you more credibility than your knowledge of your own products, so be customer-focused and flow in your pitch.

Chapter 6

Leverage

Customers may say no, even when the presentation is great and the solution offers a sure win for them. People are creatures of habit, and your customers may be reluctant and afraid to part with their old ways. Why? The reasons are many, both real and perceived.

Hansel, a senior key-account manager, is an eloquent presenter whose presentations have always received a positive reception. Some new customers have actually signed on the dotted line instantly. Most customers, however, asked for more time to review the presentation in a separate discussion.

I remember Hansel well because he always complained that fickle customers created more problems for him by demanding better counter arguments, case studies, and visual presentations. He found that despite his diligence in refining his presentations, however, most customers still insisted on asking more questions. They challenged his recommendations and even insisted on more documented explanation. He was irritated by the additional work and couldn't figure out where the problem lay!

What's in It for Me?

The French mathematician and philosopher Blaise *Pascal said,* "People are generally better persuaded by the reasons which they have themselves discovered than by those which have come into the mind of others." *Pascal's* quote aptly explains Hansel's problem. What Pascal meant was that people almost invariably arrive at their beliefs, not on the basis of proof, but on the basis of what makes sense to *them*. In Hansel's case, unless he helps customers to persuade themselves that his proposal matches their needs, all further presentation is futile.

Hansel has lost many opportunities by taking his customers head-on without giving them breathing space to allow for self-reasoning. In Hansel's eyes, it was a zero-sum game—his customers' response must be a definite black and white, yes or no, right up front. But was he right? Not at all. Hansel's method of pressing the solution into their hands put them off, and they rejected his offers. The missing ingredient in his close was that the customers were not given an outlet to truly consider and persuade themselves that Hansel's solutions were right for *them*.

Imagine the number of missed opportunities Hansel has suffered throughout his career! Fortunately, he has since learned how essential it is to leverage the feedback after a presentation, both in dialogue and disagreement.

The Awkward Silence

If customers feel uncomfortable with giving feedback, they may decide not to share anything with you. When you reach this brick wall of silence, you've got a problem.

I once spent an entire session with a nonprofit governing body for voluntary welfare associations. Their task was to implement a new corporate governance that would give greater accountability to the corporate donors of charity funds. While the requirement was mandated and no buy-in was needed, they found that their proposal resulted in shoddy compliance to the new policies.

The focus of our session was to help them understand why their proposal to their stakeholders received a lukewarm response or no response at all. After some discussion, the governing body realized that underneath the stony silence, there were lots of unanswered questions that the audience had failed to ask because of a reluctance to open and share their *real* concern.

What do you do when you get dead silence after a presentation? The customers have been attentive throughout, but now they simply don't say anything at all. You're wondering what happened as the cold air permeates the room.

Some cultures in Asia—being non-confrontational in nature—prefer to provide feedback some time after the official presentation. What that means for you is that you've got to arrange for one-to-one appointments with the key decision makers at a later date.

If you're aware of the cultural difference and want to warm up that segment of the discussion, then take a short recess or even a tea break. Don't disappear, but mingle with your customers and solicit their feedback. They may feel more relaxed and open up toward you during the break.

But what do you do if the room stays silent? Look for body language suggesting that someone is eager to ask a question and ask them if they will start the segment with a question. That often spurs others to ask questions too.

Another way of breaking the silence is to plant questions with customers who have been positive and receptive throughout your presentation. If you choose this method, plan your questions so that their answers will place you in a favorable position and reinforce the value of your proposal.

Sometimes, you need to guide your customers along with an opening question. For example, you can show a slide containing commonly asked questions to trigger some thinking. Give them a few minutes to digest the slide, and then ask them if there are any questions that they would like answered.

Is the Presentation Enough?

Whether your customers are reluctant to share or demand even more detailed information, the moral of the story is this: delivering a killer presentation isn't about the race to the finished line without interruptions.

Why can't the presentation close the deal instantly? If you've done an excellent presentation with an excellent proposal that addresses the customers' needs, isn't resistance a sign that you've lost the deal? No.

It's natural for customers to have doubts and worries as they enter their self-searching mode, whether they express it through silence or a barrage of questions. In fact, be suspicious if the customer tells you that he is totally sold without questions—his quick acceptances could result in regret later on.

That's why it's imperative to take advantage of the self-searching mode to show your customers that you are still the trusted choice for them.

Leverage—the *L* in FIREFLY

Even the most professional sales presentation may be met with objections from the prospect, but it may have nothing to do with the actual presentation. In fact, it's more likely a simple matter of human psychology. Nobody likes to be told what to do, whether it's at home, at work, or in a presentation. In truth, it's surprising that you don't run into *more* hesitation, ambivalence, or resistance from your customers.

Unfortunately, most sales opportunities and conflicts arrive at a stalemate because both parties adopt a defensive stance. Many of us are like Hansel—impatient to nip the objection in the bud, we rush to provide answers and reinforce our pitch, hoping to impress our customers further. This is hardly the way to resolve a deadlock or dissention.

Deadlocks happen because there is no common ground between the parties due to their opposing views. One is trying to sell his idea, and the other is trying to push it away. Nobody gives in, and it becomes a challenge to reconcile divergent views.

How does one mesh viewpoints and create a common ground? The answer: *stop* trying to persuade and coax the other party. That is no longer conducive to reaching a settlement. Stop selling and start searching to *understand* the other party instead.

No matter how convincing your proposition may be, after it's done, you need to focus on the audience's emotions and thought patterns. This is a phase we call leverage. To *leverage* means to take advantage of any feedback even, and especially, dissention and disagreement.

To *leverage* means to turn conflict into a safe sharing environment. In the leverage engagement, you should seek to understand the customer instead of expecting the customer to understand you.

In the leverage phase of FIREFLY, it is time to stop the instinctive impulse to answer back and reason out every concern. Instead, stay calm and attentive. Allow the silence to permeate the room if the customer needs some time to digest the proposal. Observe your customer's body language and begin to reconnect by encouraging him to ask you questions for further clarification. Focus on understanding the customers' feedback and clarifying his uncertainty and doubts. Leverage your customer's objection—they are testing your conviction and the credibility of your proposal.

Relating back to the charity governing board, the way for them to leverage the silent resistance is to create a safe outlet for sharing. Unless they are able to encourage their stakeholders to express hidden concerns, there will be no opportunity to resolve those concerns.

Ask and You Shall Receive, Seek and You Shall Find

Entertaining questions will not, as some mistakenly think, hem you in. Receiving questions is a cornerstone to instilling open dialogue.

First, what you said during your presentation may not be what your customer heard or understood. Everyone absorbs and interprets information differently, and the same conclusion can be derived from two different logic flows from two different people. When you encourage questions, you get feedback and know where your customers are coming from.

Second, by allowing questions, you let the customer release any pent-up disagreement with your content—disagreement that you can then rectify.

Importantly, by engaging the customers to participate and speak up, you have also transformed the *deadlock* into a *dialogue*. It's a win-win situation because your customers get to ask and clarify, and you get a chance to understand and answer in return.

So if you're willing to listen, you'll be able to leverage the knowledge and turn your customer's objections into opportunities. By listening well, you'll also save time by avoiding the need for inaccurate guesswork.

Be the Cornerstone of Calm When Answering Questions

Expect the customer to attack you, devalue your proposal, and challenge your proposal. They are, in fact, testing you. Unkind words and irrational comments may be hurled at you, but maintain your best behavior when handling difficult questions.

When questions are asked, stay calm, and show your earnest desire to help the customer clarify his doubts or concern. Maintain eye contact and nod to show that you're attentive. Avoid shaking your head or frowning as if to imply you are not pleased. Never interrupt the customer when he is speaking and always allow him to complete his sentence. If speaking with a panel, don't lose focus on the rest of the audience when responding to one customer.

Make sure that you understand the question fully before answering and clarify again if you're unclear. You can also begin by paraphrasing the customer's question and then checking to see if it is correct.

Most important, stay positive, and keep in mind that his questions may well stem from a genuine desire to understand you further!

Handling Difficult Feedback after a Presentation

Experienced customers sometimes use tactics to scare and challenge you. Don't be alarmed if conversations get challenging or even personal. Remember not to take it personally, and don't get upset when things begin to get a bit tense during the discussion.

At times, the customers may be brutal and cold in their responses. Even when you reply and explain, they may still shake their head or frown intently. What then should you do?

Understand the dynamics of the decision-making team so that you can respond accordingly. If this is a decision maker, you've got to answer his questions and not avoid them. Be ready to answer and to ask questions in return when unsure. Be honest and ask for extra time if you don't have the answer on hand.

One thing you should *never* do is to blatantly say, "Mr. Julius, I can see that you don't agree with my response. Why is that so?" This will put the customer in a defensive mode. When faced with objections, the last thing you want is a debate and a war of words.

Handling objections and dissention are essential as they may reflect information we have missed out during the course of our presentation.

Several personalities may appear during a difficult meeting.

Here are some common awkward situations that you'll need to handle when your customers are drilling you with questions:

Dominant Daisy: A Dominant Daisy customer is characterized by incessant and often irrelevant questions. These questions are used to dilute the value of your proposal without a clear reason.

Handling Dominant Daisy requires you to keep a watchful eye for the signs of other members appearing weary and distracted when she continues to attack you. In a pragmatic, non-confrontational way, check with them if Dominant Daisy's questions also resonate with them and if her interrogation is an exception or a norm. In this way, you can prioritize the importance of her questions while recognizing the importance of using her peers to respond. It is important to garner their view on her questions; if her aggressive style of asking misleading questions is a norm, then you'll know that you should treat her with polite tact without allowing yourself to become too affected by her confrontational style.

Whispering William: He is seen having side conversations and whispering with his colleagues seated next to him as you are speaking. Don't embarrass him by asking his views head-on like "Mr. Kipling, do you have something to share?"

This might be too confrontational or embarrassing for him.

Instead, you might start by standing a little closer to him to see if he relents with his sideline chitchats and stops his whispering act.

However, if he continues, you could begin by asking him a general question about something you just spoke about. For example, "Mr. Kipling, what's your opinion on solar energy as an alternative source of energy?" Be tactful you're your tone and by now, you will have him responding to you directly.

Aggressive Arnold: Aggressive Arnold is direct, blunt, and does not mince his words. He is quick to judge and tries to put you in a defensive mode. Don't be shaken by his quick, brutally honest words, but stay composed and confident as he interrogates you. Acknowledge his views and gently explain your differing approach. Conclude with a common ground comprising shared values to reinforce the relevance of your point.

At junctures where opinions may strongly differ, simply agree to disagree. In these cases use phrases like "There's more than one way to skin a cat" to associate with problem solving, or "All roads still lead to Rome" to demonstrate common ground even when views differ.

If the aggressive customer's demands fall outside of the agenda, show your sincerity in addressing his question by suggesting a dedicated discussion later. For example, you could reply by saying, "That's an excellent question, but we're running on a tight schedule, and I need more time to elaborate on our business model. Can I get together with you after this presentation to show you how we have done it in the past?"

When you face questions, remember that they could be manifestations of fears, uncertainties, and doubts. It is up to you to keep the climate warm and friendly regardless of the customer's aggression. Your goal is to encourage him to speak up so that you'll know how to respond the way they want you to.

Moving from Negative to Neutral

All objections are actually questions in disguise. Our job is to turn the objection into a question in the prospect's mind so we can answer it and move them from negative to neutral gear. At this stage, resistance or disbelief could be the cry of the customer. Coming down too strongly could turn off the customer.

Instead, take control of the conversation so that you can bridge the concern by uncovering the issues at heart. You want to assure the customer that you are on his side and have his interests covered.

When a customer disagrees or is doubtful about your presentation, don't try to get him on the positive side too quickly, as he may need time to sort out his thoughts and your counterarguments. Instead, be patient and sieve out the genuine concerns so you can address them. If you can address his concerns, you will have hit jackpot because you have shifted him from negative to neutral gear. Only then can you continue your pitch, in the hopes of progressing to positive gear.

Applying the ARISE Tool to Create Common Ground

Use the ARISE method to move from no to neutral:

Acknowledge: When a customer says "No, I disagree with your concept," acknowledge his right to his opinion by responding, "Yes, I can see what you mean."

Reflect: Summarize to show you fully understand what he's saying, "So what you mean is that you prefer the previous approach because it is a tried-and-tested formula. Is that correct?" By parroting what he has said, you show the customer that you understand what he said.

Inquire: Once he confirms that you are on the same wavelength with him, you can proceed to clarify. If he appears cold, seek permission to ask the question first: "Would you mind if I ask a question to understand further?" Or just ask the question directly: "May I ask you about the extended lead time needed to complete the project with the current option?" You don't want to make assumptions; you want to clarify and confirm. Your aim is to understand the reason or motive behind the position taken.

Suggest: Once you understand the intentions behind the position taken, you can then proceed to suggest or expand on your pitch. Take note of what is important to your customer so you can pitch an idea that is congruent with the customer's point of view.

Empathize: Empathy is the ability to put yourself in the prospect's shoes without becoming emotionally involved. The purpose of empathizing is to make the prospect feel relaxed and connected with you. Let the prospect know that you are on his side. In turn, as you listen to his priorities, be ready to shape your explanation according to what he values. When you empathize, your pitch moves away from your proposition, allowing you instead to relate to the information he shares with you.

Be conscious that every customer needs to mitigate risk, especially if they are working on a very important project or a new vendor. Show empathy for this concern, and demonstrate your commitment to reducing those risks for him.

Apply ARISE when your customer is in negative gear so he can gradually move to neutral mode. Once he is in neutral mode, he will be more open to your suggestions.

End with the Beginning in Mind

Remember that the customer only wants to know "What is in it for me?" Therefore, when you conclude your session, it's important to end on a positive note about the value your organization can bring to him.

Concluding with a short feedback session will allow both parties to create more understanding between each other. In addition, you'll enlarge the pie by discovering differences and more reasons to work together.

Summary

Handling feedback is the heart of a presentation. Customers need to take time to digest your presentation. When your customer gives feedback, remember to stay open and receptive to their opinions.

Welcoming questions allows your customer to air his views, concerns, and doubts. Knowing his concerns and doubts will bring you closer to knowing him.

At times you may be faced with difficult and awkward situations. When that happens, stay focused on the customer's needs. Realize that you may not have all the answers because there may be some hidden or unexplained needs. Remain calm and collected as you collect feedback to address those needs.

In the event of silence, use the ARISE technique to gently coax questions and feedback from the customers. Never take no as an end to the conversation, but intentionally move the conversation forward with ARISE so you can explore and uncover more about the customer's needs. The more information you gather, the stronger position you'll be in to sharpen your pitch and shape your response. Unless there is dialogue, there will only be a deadlock.

Chapter 7

Yield

Have you ever been to a meeting that starts on a positive note, sizzles into an interactive engagement midway, and then ends with an ambivalent "maybe"? It's a terrible feeling. To make matters worse, when we're unable to get an acceptance from the customer, we often give up too easily. The final section of the FIREFLY consultative-engagement phase is how to get around this and turn it to your advantage. Welcome to "Yield."

When we conclude our discussions after an intense display of how we're going to make a difference, we're trained to go for the jugular and ask for the sale. Our instinctive hunter impulse says, "Collect a signed contract!" But while the adage "If you don't ask, you don't get" may hold true, concluding a meeting with a "my way or the highway" approach may not augur well for either the customer or you. Why? The problem with written proposals is that they can look extremely similar to each other during the proposal phase, so customers get confused because there seems to be little difference between the competitors.

Because customers have what seem to be identical options, the sophisticated ones aren't going to stop at what you have to offer. Having gone through other vendors, the customer is well aware that the power to say no is a powerful negotiation tool.

Using Closing Techniques May Still Work

You are told never to leave the customer waiting too long to make a decision lest he changes his mind. Or that your customer should never be in such control of the conversation that he is able to take his time with the decision. Instead, you're expected to motivate him to move forward, regardless of a positive, negative, or neutral stand from the customer.

To a certain extent, you'll still have to encourage the customer to sign and accept the agreement if both parties have achieved full clarity and understanding about all outstanding issues, but even in this case, your *bigger* goal is to ensure that the customer likes you and your company.

Be Closing from the Start, Not at the End

Mildred is one of the top key-account managers in her male-dominated industry. What's surprising about her is that contrary to the aggressive stereotype of top managers, she is soft-spoken and mild-mannered.

When I asked her her secret to becoming a top sales professional for five consecutive years running was, she told me that she counts herself lucky to have a good set of clients who are always open despite being demanding and tough. She even remarked on how her most resistant customers have become her best teachers.

At the beginning, I was surprised by her comment. But when she shared with me how she eventually succeeded in managing her more demanding customers, I understood how the paradox paid off for her handsomely.

Her most demanding customers taught her to pay more attention to their expectations. Even if she were selling the same product to different customers, the needs and priorities were markedly different.

For example, two years ago, she had just completed a difficult presentation. The proposal had been challenged despite its vast offering of attractive option. This was because this account had been marred by a spate of unfortunately events and service failures.

Mildred, ever the astute observer, recalled how her boss would ask the customer for a partial acceptance of the proposal, only to be received with cold shoulders because they were not ready to sign. She realized from her years of working with corporate customers that they often still want more after they have made you their vendor of choice. Even with the best-value proposition, they will work even harder to get more out of you.

So Mildred took time after the meeting to arrange for a one-to-one meeting with each member of the decision-making committee to address their issues and garner support for the deal.

Mildred's secret to finally wrapping up the deal was the time she had spent to understand the reasons why the customer short-listed her in the first place despite the poor track record. By capitalizing on what the customer valued in her, she increased her chances of being chosen as the final vendor by anticipating the areas that the customers cared most about. To Mildred, closing the deal was about finding out how to reassure the customer throughout the entire engagement. She would comb through every concern that they had and would move quickly to address it.

Closing well meant that her customers must find her patient, knowledgeable, and sensitive to their needs. Mildred has earned the trust and approval of her clients because she perseveres in uncovering every single concern, big or small. She had learnt that winning the customers was as direct as taking the time to settle all doubts so that she can anticipate their future needs better.

How *Not* to Close

Nicole, on the other hand, is a case study of what not to do. Nicole was a feisty and aggressive sales rookie who never took no for an answer. While she too was a top performer, customers frequently rated her as abrasive and hard in her sales approach, especially as she would come down hard at the final moment to close the deal.

But wait a second. Is aggressiveness not an important trait for a salesperson?

Yes, it is—and customers were admittedly impressed by her gusto and determination. With typical gusto, she would solicit feedback from her support team and return with more information to show her customers how her company measured up against the competition. She was quick to address and eliminate every objection raised by the customer.

However, even as the customers yielded to her recommendations, they felt smothered by her. She just came on too strongly with her aggressive closing offers. Sure they bought from her—but only once. Her brashness destroyed further sales potential.

These days, customers are no push-over for old-fashioned predictable closing tricks—that means no more hard sell tactics and tactical closing lines.

Instead, customers want you to listen to them and give them what they want before they say yes. They want to be the ones who decide and not to have it pushed on them by you. The customer's sentiments are aptly summed up in "I will buy, but only because I want to, not because you told me to."

For your part, you have to yield to them. But how do you yield without giving up too much control?

Yield—the *Y* in FIREFLY

When customers expect you to yield to their demands, they want what is best for their organization. They want the assurance that their interests have been taken into account once they say yes to your proposal.

All customers feel a sense of vulnerability. They feel exposed when they show signs of preferring your proposal to the competition. That's why most of the time they prefer not to show their delight during your presentation. Instead, they slow down, feign disinterest, or grill you further to test your mettle.

In the yield phase of FIREFLY, show your allegiance to the customer by giving them the notion that they have won a larger piece of the pie. The point is to make them feel at closing as if their grilling caused you to yield them a very favorable deal. Customers need to feel that we have yielded to their calls for more flexibility, options, or leeway. When they have the sense that they have been leading the conversation, they'll feel like it's a win-win outcome for both sides. When we yield to the customer, what we're doing is giving up the notion that our solution is the definitive answer to their needs. Instead, we're reaffirming our creed that our customers are number one.

In Nicole's situation, her aggressive nature made her customers feel that she was being too high-handed. No matter how great your solution is, customers need to feel that they are the alpha dog.

Nicole should have made her customers feel secure with her by learning how to give-and-take when concluding a sale. Importantly, she had to learn to close a meeting by demonstrating a dual benefit for both parties. Placing her solutions on a pedestal for the customer is not enough. They need to *know* that they got the best deal in the end.

Understanding the Customer's Vulnerability

At the end of any presentation, your customers' views can vary for many reasons. As many of us are impatient to nip the objection in the bud, we rush to provide answers and reinforce our pitch, hoping to impress our customers further.

The trouble is that the decision can be distressing for the customer and cause him to regret his decision. Even when faced with a good proposal, he may experience cold feet or an impulse to slow down and even backtrack. After all, commitment is tough, and the wrong decision can be devastating to one's personal or professional interest. As such, you've got to yield to his concerns and address them during the closing phase.

What's so unnerving about making that final decision?

1. The customer may be unnerved by the finality of his decision.
2. The customer has to accept not only the advantages, but also the possible disadvantages associated with their selection.
3. By not choosing the other vendors, the customer has literally given up all potential to experience the possible benefits of the other

options. It's the little "What if?" voice that jolts him and leads him to question himself.

So when it comes to the crunch time, sometimes we need to allow the customer to slow down the decision-making process and reverse the search for comparative information. Only in this way can he finally be convinced that his choice is the right one.

The more risky the project or the more similar the alternative options are, the tougher it becomes for him to decide.

How to Move from Dissonance to Decision

Once you notice that the customer is putting on the breaks and citing possible scenarios that need reevaluation, be ready to reduce the dissonance that comes from making a decision.

Here are some ways to reduce the possibility of regret in the decision making stage:

- Increase the attractiveness of your proposal. Relate your proposal to issues that are close to your customer's heart, thus contextualizing the proposal and increasing its relevance. Align the outcome to your customer's personal and professional motives.
- Highlight the *distinct and differentiated edge* your solution has over the competition's.
- Devalue alternative options by emphasizing the criteria essential in achieving the customer's desired outcome. Cite the agreed criteria and objectively explain how your competitors' options pale in comparison to yours.

Instead of criticizing the competitors, stay professional by explaining the gap between your competencies versus the others. In the customer's eye, you have objectively helped him understand why he is justified in eliminating that option.

It is of utmost importance to soothe your customer's fear of regret by reinforcing to him that by choosing you over the rest, he will be making a decision that is most consistent with his motives.

Handling the Irrational Customer Gently

Irrationality is driven by emotion. Research has proven that customers do make decisions emotionally and then rationalize them afterward.

Some customers use emotions as a way to test you. Before you can handle such a situation, you've got to know your agreed zone for negotiation and at which point you will walk away. Without a clear position, you may find yourself at the losing end, but by knowing your own limits, you won't end up in a yo-yo conversation with the customer.

Never argue with an irrational customer as you might be dealing with reasons unrelated to the practical aspects. Emotional elements may include a perceived trust with an existing long-term vendor or distrust with you.

Perhaps there is a degree of bias toward another option despite convincing evidence that you are the right choice. In that case, it's a perception issue for you to grapple with. Don't discredit perception issues—perceptions shape reality.

Moving from Facts to Feelings

Stop the factual debate and move toward building the relationship and improving your rapport with the customer instead. Find out what their personal motives are—they might include his need for recognition, how a future promotion hinges on the success of this project, or simply that he needs to be seen as the boss.

Perhaps you may want to offer an opportunity to meet with him separately in order to get to know him at a personal level. It's always good to step outside of the cold meeting room and catch up one-to-one. Find a relaxing environment so the customer will be comfortable enough to open up to you.

Yielding to the Customer's Needs with Weapons of Influence

Being persuasive right through to the end of the pitch is crucial. The more influential you are, the higher the chance that the customer will create a positive opportunity with you.

The following techniques can help you in your approach as you move toward the close of the conversation. Robert Cialdini, in his book on persuasion, defined six weapons of influence. Wielding these weapons deftly will create a positive opportunity for the customer to choose yes in the final phase of the sales engagement.

Reciprocity: People tend to return a favor. Do a good deed even before the deal is signed. And while you're at it, take the opportunity to show them what you can do for them. By doing so, your proactive approach could trigger a positive impression in the customer to work with you in future. For example, you might perform a small task on a complimentary basis to show how fast your response time is. When you do, be sure to position it the right way with your customer: "We have provided a complimentary consultation for one of the sales teams, and we're glad to hear that they were able to fix the bug in their software system. It's something we routinely use, so it's free of charge to you."

Commitment and consistency: Once people commit to what they think is right, they are more likely to honor that commitment. For example, as you recall the customer's opinions and preferences, your pitch should stay relevant to what he has said before. Say it right: "Mr. Lewis, as you have mentioned that you prefer to work on a project-based approach with minimal level of investment in machinery, the leasing recommendation will help you reduce capital expenditure by 45 percent, and that's 10 percent more than your current supplier can offer you."

Likewise, since people are unlikely to contradict themselves, be sure to seek the customer's commitment throughout your pitch.

Social proof: People will do things that they see other people doing. For example, provide assurance by using the newspapers to show how companies are turning to biofuel as a cost-effective alternative to energy utilization. Say it right: "Did you know that 40 percent of Fortune 1000 companies are already using this approach? Here's a recent newspaper article that talks about the successes of some of the companies in Asia who have company scales similar to yours."

This evidence provides assurance that they are consistent with market trends. But make sure that your reference is relevant to their business or a best practice that can be adopted regardless of industry type.

Authority: People will tend to obey figures in authority even if the decision is something that they don't like. For example, leaders like Niemen Marcus and Tiffany's—originally confined to retail shops only—are now moving toward online shopping for customers. This trend might be ushering in a new approach for those thinking of preserving their distribution margins. Say it right: "The CEO of Niemen Marcus launched their prestigious online web store last year. This was a strategic move that allowed them to keep up with changing customer needs in the Internet space."

Lean on credible third-party references that the customer respects to ink your deal. Show them how confident others have been with your performance and outcome.

Liking: People are easily persuaded by people they like. Remember to flex to the different personality types as well as being relevant to the customer. Be likeable!

Scarcity: Perceived scarcity will generate demand. For example, saying a discount is valid for seven days will create a sense of urgency to take advantage of this one-time opportunity. Nobody wants to lose out on a good offer! Say it right: "If you commit today, we'll extend our promise to ensure stock availability for the next thirty days. This product is the best seller in our range, but we've gone out of our way to extend this offer to you!"

Mesh these techniques during your final closing so that you can influence the customers toward commitment in a professional manner.

Concession—Give to Get

Before a commitment is given, some customers—especially, I have found, those in Asia—like to haggle before giving their final acceptance. Come with your concession ready in your mind so you can close the opportunity without giving more than you want.

But don't give concessions away for free. Give pragmatic concessions when you see a customer who is genuinely interested in the deal. And keep in mind that these concessions should cater to the customers' needs.

Give Concessions Without Diluting Your Value

There are two ways that to explain the give-to-get approach. Focus either on (*a*) the gain that your customer can realize or (*b*) the pain that he can avoid or mitigate. When you yield to his needs with a concession, you are asking for a commitment to let you help him achieve his goal.

Justify with the Minimax Approach

A concession, when used at the right time along with the right message, places you in the right light with your customer. In turn, a concession is deemed meaningful if you can do the minimax; that is, *minimize* his pain and *maximize* his gain while offering the concession as a closing goodwill gesture.

Here are a couple examples to get you started on minimaxing:

Minimum pain: "If you can commit today, we'll make an exception and process the documents over the weekend so you can have coverage and peace of mind. No other insurance organization can do this for you. Would you prefer the elite or the premium coverage for next week's event?"

Maximum gain: "You'll improve your response rate by 20 percent if you start with us today. If you commit today, we'll reciprocate by giving you a one-time 5 percent discount. Which database would you like for us to work on for phase one?"

Finally, if you have given the fifty-fifty split down the middle, use that as the final closing concession. This approach is best used to demonstrate an equal commitment from both parties in the final round.

When doing so, say it right: "John, I'm willing to meet you halfway because I really want us to start working on this order right away. If you can increase the volume purchase by forty thousand units instead of twenty thousand units, we're willing to give you the discounted price you requested. That will mean a savings of more than 14 percent from our original proposal."

Don't forget to stay alert for chances to give concessions to show the customer you are committed to creating a win-win situation for both sides.

What If He Says No?

Customers say no as much as or more than they say yes. In the case of a rejection, don't take it personally. Think of ways to repackage the offer to a size that works for him. Alternatively, you may attempt to get commitment for a partial section of the proposal instead.

If the customer really puts his foot down and gives you a definite no, take the opportunity to invest in the future by understanding the reasons for his current negative decision. Never take no to mean never.

In addition, go beyond and ask if you can stay in touch with him. Take advantage of your customer-relationship marketing system, and include him as a contact so he will stay on your prospecting list. Instead of a lost client, view this as a valuable addition to your contact database.

Summary

We have been trained to seal the deal and lock the customer in at the close. In reality, however, if you don't stay focused on what the customer truly wants, you can easily end up offering deals that don't meet the customer's needs—thereby devaluing your original proposal.

One thing to note is that the final decision is never easy for the customer, especially if there is an incumbent vendor that he's been used to for some time. Bear in mind that moving over to a new untested solution may pose risks to his professional credibility and, perhaps, his personal image.

Understanding how to minimize post-decision regrets can help alleviate the customer's anxiety in his decision-making process. Emphasizing the edge you hold above your competitors does count. The more you can justify your competitive edge, the more assured the customer will feel.

Don't forget to use the weapons of influence to guide the way you communicate while staying rooted and relevant to the customer's needs. When using concessions, do so in an appropriate manner so that you don't devalue your proposition.

Use options to increase your chances of getting a yes response. Be creative, and give the customer more choices should he indicate a preference for a different approach. Your creativity will allow him more flexibility to agree with certain parts of the proposal, if not all.

Finally, when you conclude a meeting, create a powerful impression by staying confident that you are bringing a solution of good value to the customer. A good close is one that yields to a win-win solution for both sides. You give the customer the assurance that he has the best offering, and your customer chooses you because you have given him a strong reason to make that commitment without regret.

Chapter 8

Putting It Together

One can never underestimate the power of engagement. While many books throughout the years have expounded on different approaches to sales engagement, simplicity and relevance are the keys to accessing today's customers.

It's not only what you do in the sales engagement that counts, it's how you say it and when you say it too. In a market where customers are sophisticated and more demanding than ever, a relationship based on cold hard selling alone just won't win and keep customers anymore.

The customer wants you to have *both* style and substance. This multifaceted demand raises the bar for anybody who needs to be convincing and credible in front of an unknown audience. If you are able to develop a systematic approach during your conversations, you'll bring out the best in your customer relationships. This is especially true during your crucial first encounter.

In their jointly authored book *The Art of Woo*, G. Richard Shell and Mario Moussa lay out a four-step approach to strategic persuasion. They explain that the purpose of persuasion is not to *defeat* the other party but rather to *win over* the other party.

Recognizing the validity of this approach, this book is written as an engagement tool to help not just sales professionals but anyone who needs to pitch an idea or an opinion. This book will give you a look at consultative engagement from a different angle.

How to use this book, you ask? Although I initially designed it as a sequential seven-step approach to a winning sales engagement, some of my clients have approached it from a modular approach, choosing to focus only on specific areas of pressing need at any one point in time. To really take advantage of the power of this book, I suggest you start from the beginning to raise your self-awareness first, and then proceed to sharpen your engagement afterward.

FIREFLY—Systematic and Easy to Remember

Why FIRE?

You need to FIRE before you can FLY. The FIRE engagement approach is the initial phase. It focuses on a proactive question-based conversation to understand the customer's situation, goals, and challenges.

Customers are less likely to be open with people they are not comfortable with, so remove the arm's-length discussion and transform it into a comfortable and mutually beneficial relationship. Seek to understand the customer's world and their perspective of the issues in that world. Only when you fully understand the customer's requirements from his perspective can you confidently present a solution guaranteed to appeal to them.

The FIRE phase creates instant credibility for you when you come armed with the right words and the finesse to ask delicate questions effortlessly. Your personality will become magnetic, and customers will feel drawn when you build rapport with them.

Why FLY?

Thereafter, FLY works in tandem with FIRE—and both are instrumental in bringing out the best in a relationship. The FLY engagement phase focuses on making a solid pitch. This pitch addresses not only your customers' professional requirements, but is also sensitive to their personal and emotional needs. After all, most decisions are made on the basis of perception, past experiences, and even intuition.

During FLY, you'll see why stumbling blocks during a pitch are not bad; they are actually good. They present an opportunity to understand issues that were missed out. When handled well, you can turn those issues into a solution in which nothing is missed out. Finally, FLY concludes with the need to uphold the relationship by focusing on closing it optimally—either with a solid commitments or a warm relationship if the customer's final decision is negative.

Quick Review of the FIREFLY Seven-Step Approach

Flex. Understand by asking or observing the response of individuals you meet. Make an initial assessment of their personality style (two styles normally show up at a time), and flex to their style, modulating the speed, pace, and your choice of words.

Impress. Impress customers by coming prepared for the meeting and presenting yourself in a professional yet approachable manner. Ensure that your body language, tone of voice, and choice of words are synchronized to portray confidence and attentiveness.

Rapport. Creating small talk, no matter how small, helps you to warm up the initial meeting by breaking the ice. Come prepared with views and questions for both a casual chitchat and a more serious business-focus topic based on the other party's preference.

Engage. This is the art of creating an interactive session. Employing active listening skills and empathy, you will uncover the customer's needs—even if they're unsaid. Your advance preparation of essential questions will minimize the time spent and help you better prepare for the proposal.

Flow. The only way to present with impact is to flow with the customer's business needs and context. Make sure your ideas are aligned to the customer's values by echoing back what they have said to you. The more you sound like the customer, the more believable your proposal will sound.

Leverage. Customer resistance and objections are instrumental to any selling engagement because they create an opportunity to understand and dialogue further. Stay positive and listen well to unmet needs so you can review and resolve them the second time around!

Yield. When you close a discussion, lead the customer to a commitment by showing your own commitment to a win-win for both parties. Sophisticated customers want to know they have made the right decision. Construct options and concessions so that you can create more opportunities for customers to say yes. And even if they say no, find out why, and keep them on your radar for down the road.

Be the Light for Your Customers

FIREFLY will give you the confidence to bring out the best in your business relationships with your customer and help you gain trust fast with any prospect.

Equipped with these engagement tools, you'll begin to lead rather than sell.

Go forth and be the light for your customers!

Index